Empowerment
of
Man and Woman

Channeled by

Nancy R. Griffin

authorHOUSE®

AuthorHouse™
1663 Liberty Drive
Bloomington, IN 47403
www.authorhouse.com
Phone: 1-800-839-8640

First published by AuthorHouse 11/3/2011

ISBN: 978-1-4670-6266-4 (e)
ISBN: 978-1-4670-6267-1 (sc)

Printed in the United States of America

Any people depicted in stock imagery provided by Thinkstock are models,
and such images are being used for illustrative purposes only.
Certain stock imagery © Thinkstock.

This book is printed on acid-free paper.

Introduction

This section is being written for you, the Sons of God whom have lost their way. I am your Father and your Mother from Higher Realm. We are dictating these truths because the sons of God have separated themselves from us. They have become the sons of Earth.

You, whom even attempt to love us and attend your religious Churches, Temples, Synagogues have also separated from us. Performing religious ceremonies instead of aligning with us, you pray as parrots, chant as parrots. Your hearts are filled with judgment.

You, whom have stepped away from any form of worship, have filled your heart with earthly pleasures. Men have forgotten that they were made to be physically stronger, so they may protect and support the female. We will help you return to your god-selves, through true prayer within, through true alignment with us, ending war, murder, adultery, and greed. We will end the diet of death and transform your life with the diet of life resulting in divine marriages and families.

There are duplicate chapters in both sections of this book (Empowerment of Man and Empowerment of Woman) because the information applies to both men and women. The duplicate chapters are: The Valiant Ones, The Sins of the Father Fall upon the Son, The Dark, and Prophecies for the Future.

Table of Contents

CHAPTER I

Misunderstanding the Word

There are many misunderstandings of the words in the Bible. We have listed some of the misunderstandings in other chapters, but we feel by placing all of them in one chapter it will be easier for you to recall.

To love God with all thy might! Means to align with us and our love will support you in all your life and existence. We will intervene and support you.

To love thy neighbor as thyself! This means to recognize the life-force within you and also recognize the life-force in all others, giving you the true understanding that all Creation is one. This is what Jesus meant when He said, *"Mother, brother, sister, we are all one and the same."* All living matter is of the Creator, of Creation. To love thy neighbor as thyself is to recognize the God within you, in all living beings and all living creatures. Visualize the rainbow fused light in all living matter, hold that picture in your mind, allow it to imprint, then you will be able to love thy neighbor as thyself. Those of you, whom try to love an earthly limited, personal love, struggle with this Commandment. It cannot be done by attempting to emotionally love your neighbor. You will fail because some of your neighbors are very unpleasant neighbors. By you recognizing the Source of Light within them, you are acknowledging the Creator within them – that is all that is required of you. It removes you from judgment.

In the beginning was the word, and the word was God and the word was with God. This means: in the beginning of Creation there was consciousness and the consciousness was good. Love and the consciousness were positive, good, and with

1

God. This was when man knew he was part of God. God used to be spelled with two o's. It was the scribes whom changed our name to God instead of good. In the beginning all was good and love. All of you must know that all you have to do is join your Mother and I in our unconditional love. We will be awaiting you.

Let us discuss the continued misunderstanding of your vows of marriage. Oh, the misdeeds and cruelty, even murder with this misinterpretation.

The man who misused the word obey for suppression, misuse of power, control and violence will suffer from the sowing of their dark seeds. When the word <u>obey</u> was placed in the wedding vows, it was misused by men of ill intent. The word obey means: to <u>align with</u>, NOT to submit to the misuse of power. Man, did you not realize you must cherish your wife? How can you take a vow to cherish your wife and then suppress her at the same time?

You, whom have suppressed your wives and lowered yourselves to harm them, will suffer the suppression ten-fold in return. Man, if you have not cherished your wives, you have broken your vows. The vows you supposedly took before God, standing before a Rabbi, Priest or Minster. Taking a vow on an altar is only done for outer world ceremony. It has very little meaning in Spirit.

For you to go within and align with us, so much so, you will draw unto you a mate that would be Heaven sent. Then you both would align with Higher Realm. And if you feel the world requires a ceremony before a Rabbi, Priest, Minister or Judge, so be it.

To go to so much 'to do' and expense regarding a wedding is for ego only. Say your vows within first, align with your Highest God, Christ-self, then you will draw in the mate chosen for you by us, your Holy Parents.

Let us discuss earthly love versus heavenly love. Earthly love is based in the physical, mental and emotional levels. Without you being aware of it, you were programmed to be attracted to a mate who reflects your programming of what love looks like from your earthly parents.

If you came from a family where your father was supportive and loving, it will be easier for you to be so (supportive and loving). If you came from a dysfunctional family, as most of you have, due to over fifty percent divorce rate, you will have a distorted program of what love looks like. If you came from a single mother home, you will either expect your wife to work or you will struggle to make ends meet by insisting your wife stays home. You must also contend with the programming your wife experienced.

If both of you came from single parent homes, the chances are very high that your marriage will not survive because you were not given the skills to experience a successful marriage. There are the families whom had both parents and the parents stayed together for all the wrong reasons, never giving their children the correct patterns for a loving marriage. You must look back to their parents (your grandparents) for how your parents were programmed.

The misunderstood words are: The sins of the father fall upon the son. This means: you, an impressionable child will follow your parent's patterns or actions and words.

How many of you heard yourselves say to your children the very negative response you heard from your parents that you swore you would never say? You were programmed into the cells of your body and subconscious. The sins of the father fall upon the son; means the programming of your parents imprint your beliefs and fears.

The word fear is also misunderstood. It means to <u>believe!</u> If you fear God, you believe in God or good, not to be afraid! Fear from your Bible means to believe. Your fears come upon you, means your beliefs manifest whatever you believe. Whatever a man thinketh of himself, so is the man. See how powerful your beliefs are. Ask and believe and it will be given unto you.

Another word that has been misinterpreted is the word <u>suffer!</u> Suffer means to allow.

"Suffer the little children to come unto me." Allow the little children to come unto me.

To suffer pain is to allow pain.

To suffer illness is to allow illness.

The true meaning is to imply you have the power of thought over all matter. The secret is to learn how to have power of your thoughts. When you stay aligned with us and Higher Realm, your thought will be empowered with unconditional love and healing. Not earthly love, but heavenly love. A love that is connected to the unlimited Source of love.

New wine is grape juice, not wine. To drink old wine, alcohol is to invite a crack in your auric shield, your life-force, leaving you open to lower form entities to drain your Light. Stay away from all carcinogens as they crack your shield!

Vengeance is mine sayeth the Lord – this was misquoted. It should read, *"Vengeance is mine sayeth the Law of Sowing and Reaping or the Law of Karma."* Whatever you give out comes back to you.

Turn the other cheek. Misunderstanding of this message has confused many. It means to literally turn your cheek and look away in consciousness. Look away from the negativity, not stand there and let someone betray you again. Turn your focus to love, to positive thoughts.

Keep your thoughts in alignment with love and Creation and you will ascend to a higher level of consciousness. The higher you go in consciousness, the more love and creativity you will experience.

To love thy neighbor as thyself – means to align with us Higher Realm, and in that recognition you will recognize the Source within all.

Another misunderstood phrase or Divine Law is: *The Kingdom of Heaven is now at hand.*

This means the only place for you to be with Creation is now! Now, this very moment. The past is only a memory and dark past deeds are not worthy of your now moment. You will just recreate the dark in your present, to go over the errors of yesterday and you will bring them into this moment.

The Kingdom of Heaven is now at hand.

It is within you, available to you. Now.

Go within, we are waiting for you.

Man, you have been told before you only have to love, protect and support. You were given a stronger physical body for your role as man. Those of you whom have separated yourselves from your inner spirit will find your role as a burden.

You will struggle, look to your source in your employment, and if you lose your employment, you will feel a failure, loss, and unworthy.

If you are in a subordinate job, you may strive to a higher position through, again, great effort on you part. When you are separated from your Spirit, you are without Universal Support. All your efforts are limited to the mental and physical realms. Life on Earth in your work force becomes a dog-eat-dog existence. Your gods are work, salary, bonuses, raises, income tax returns, insurance policies, college funds, medical, dental, etc. and this becomes your reality.

Is it any wonder that some men will turn to physical exercise in order to feel better, as it expels their endorphins, others will turn to sports, alcohol, tobacco, drugs and sex. They will do anything in order to feel a little better. They are missing the most important element in their lives – their unlimited divine Spirit. The Spirit that will fill them with all the endorphins and euphoria they are seeking through temporary means.

To breathe in the sacred breath, in a consciousness of acknowledgment of the connection, will free you, and will especially give you a supported unlimited experience of love, peace, wisdom and creative powers.

Thou shall have no other gods before me. This information is the true meaning of the misunderstood commandment – Thou shall have no other goods, loves, sources, focuses before me. You are not to kneel before a demi-god. You are to connect with the unlimited Source of life-force, which includes love, peace, wisdom, creation, prophetic knowledge, and Universal Support.

First, seek ye the Kingdom of Heaven and all other things shall be added unto you. You have heard and read this truth, but have you truly understood? No! If you had, the world would reflect that understanding. There would be peace on Earth. The brotherhood and sisterhood of man and womankind would prevail. The Buddhist or Muslims, whom chant and pray several times a day, if only they would align with us; it would be enough to shift your world. We require one hundred and forty-four thousand to align with us and it will turn the tide for Enlightenment upon Earth. All that is expected of you is to align with your Holy Mother and I, your Father daily. We will carry you through your daily life.

Another misunderstood commandant is: <u>*Honor thy Father and thy Mother.*</u>

Because your Holy Mother was removed from your Bible in the four hundred and fifties, you lost your reference to the true meaning of this commandment. To honor thy father and mother means to recognize your true self. Your true self is Spirit, and the Spirit is part of the very all. Your true self is the divine! You are our Sons. Your earthly parents became your parents to give them one opportunity to give and serve in order to be aligned with a higher consciousness. To be a parent on Earth is a commitment of love, protection and support until the age of maturity, in some cases that age is seventeen, if the child has learned to be at one with us. If the child has been weakened and always expects you or his mother to take on his responsibilities, then the child will be locked into the limited picture. If the parent has taken charge of the child's responsibilities, it will stunt the maturity of the son or daughter.

A son or daughter must develop a sense of their own maturity for them to feel good about themselves. Teach your children to go within. Give them the unlimited experience of Source.

Teach them to honor their Holy Mother and Father within them, for it will ensure not only their success and peace of mind on Earth, but also their ability to ascend to a higher consciousness after their sojourn on Earth.

It is all about bringing you home to your divine heritage and showing you the path to accomplish your ascension. The Kingdom of Heaven is within you. Go within, we are awaiting you.

<u>*Sowing and Reaping.*</u> Some of you have a small idea of what this entails. You even quote the golden rule – 'do unto others as you would have them do unto you.' You do not realize every thought, word, deed or action you express and carry out has a repercussion. It is the same as a pebble thrown into a pond. It ripples out. Take care to keep your thoughts and actions in harmony with what you wish to receive. Each thought and action are your seeds you sow. Make sure your harvest is a worthy one.

Sow the thoughts you wish to reap.

Take the actions you wish to experience.

Cast your bread upon the water, it will come back to you ten-fold.

The churches would have you believe you should tithe to them only. However, every kind word or deed is a tithing, casting your bread.

Give love and kindness and you will receive the same in return, if you also believe you are worthy of receiving. *"Whatever you think of yourself – so is the man."* If you feel and think you are unworthy of receiving, you will create lack of receiving. Your thoughts and feelings will come to pass.

Stop and reconnect with us, your Holy Parents. You will feel the expansion of your essence and realize you are worthy. You are part of the divine energy. Claim your inheritance.

Say the I am's:

I am one with Love.
I am one with God.
I am one with Peace.
I am one with unlimited grace.
Then slowly say I . . . am!

Feel the inner presence carry you to your divine path and journey. Let us support you. We are here. Align with us, your Holy Mother-Father God.

CHAPTER II

The Keys to the Kingdom

We will go back in time, hundreds of thousands of years ago; when man knew he was Spirit in the temporary form of flesh, when the Keepers of the Kingdom kept the door to Heaven open within each soul, by teaching the divine alignment on a daily basis. It was a form of inner connection to the Heaven's within.

After many years, these Keepers to the Inner Kingdom were referred to as Kings. Some of these Keepers were in female flesh and they were referred to as the feminine version of King, now known as Queen. After the destruction of many lands on Earth and the loss of this wisdom, the Keeper of Wisdom would take those on Earth to the higher level of consciousness.

The Purple Robed Masters being the lowest level of ascension are here to support us to a higher level of consciousness on our spiritual path. Next, is the White Robed Masters to the Gold, to the glorious Light White Rainbow to the Great Creator – the Great Void if you will, which is the darkest of greens.

This would be a spiritual journey and each soul on Earth would travel to the level he or she was capable of traveling to according to their ability to align with the unconditional Light of Love. So the cells of mankind's consciousness were programmed to recognize these higher levels of attainment with experiencing the colors that were reflected in that dimension.

Souls would choose to come to Earth because of the memory of past existences were mostly erased and they could start with a clean slate, to choose

Love and service. Why Earth? Because it is a lower density. It is a third density experience. For in this density, every good deed you sow, it is worth a hundred thousand good deeds on a higher level of understanding.

Souls choose Earth to advance to a higher level of expression; to become more with the Light and more with unconditional divine love.

Now, we shall address the fall of man when they lost contact with the Inner Heavens. When the Keepers of the Kingdom were taken away during the end of Atlantis, man no longer connected to the Inner Heavens. The Kingdom of Heaven that is within you had lost their Keeper of the Kingdom. Man forgot his Higher Self. He was left without guides to the inner planes.

We sent our Son and many Prophets and Avatars before and after Him, to return you to your Heaven within. But what has man done with the messages? Our Son's message to love beyond all else and the Kingdom of Heaven is within you, but did you listen?

What has man done with these messages? They have ignored the message and made a religion out of the messengers. Every church, temple or synagogue that stands on Earth looks to the messenger and not the message.

Now, let us go back to the idea of a King and Queen. They are not the Keepers of the Kingdom. They are sitting on earthly thrones with their jeweled crowns and wearing purples, gold, and white, all symbolic of the Inner Dimensions, but they are not the Keepers of the Inner Kingdom of the past. They declared war on other nations, committed adultery, executed wives that no longer suited them, taxed the people for greed, married without love to produce an heir, and then betrayed their vows for self-indulgence. They set themselves above others when in truth they have created great, massive karmic debt upon their souls. Ego has ruled royalty – ego, greed and corruption.

Take off your crowns and learn to be honest, to love and serve man and womankind. Our Son told you the first will be last and the last will be first, do you not understand?

Your crowns and robes are an abomination to the Inner Heavens. Man, womankind stop bowing down to these false Keepers to our Kingdom. When you bow or serve a false master, you are aligning yourself with their karmic debt. You have served a false god. Do you not see this?

The royal houses have lost their true way. They have become empty symbols of corruption and misuse of power. The royal house is so dark and far away from Spirit that any time a soul filled with love or service marries into the royal household, they are eliminated. The souls whom are responsible for their early deaths will carry their limited, negative karma for all eternity.

You, whom have destroyed with misuse of power, will suffer for eons and eons. Mankind has transferred his cell memory from the time of the Keeper of the Inner Kingdom, to the worship and honorment of objects of the colors of the Higher Planes. That is why gold is so worshiped, purple is considered the royal color and deep green the color of the Creator, the very all – is reflected in most of your money and currency. Silver represents the silver-white level. Your cell memory remembers these colors as a level of attainment. It is reflected in your jewelry, your worship of money, and of gold. When you are aware of your inner self, you will know that these colors are a reflection of a higher level of consciousness and spiritual attainment. They are not earthly treasures.

CHAPTER III

Temples, Synagogues and Churches

*B*efore we elaborate on these groups, we must reiterate that your body is the Temple of the Living God.

Dear Sons:

Let us discuss the true path to enlightenment. All of our Sons, Daughters, Messengers taught you the way to your God-selves, but you chose to take the path away from aligning with us and your God-selves. The dark and lower pursuits have held too much appeal.

The Book of Genesis gave you the diet of life, but most of you did not follow it. Every Avatar, Mystic, Prophet and even Christ did not eat the diet of death. They ate under the Law of Truth and ate of the Tree of Knowledge of Good only. Not of Evil.

Some of the older eastern religions follow the diet of life, but very, very few newer religions eat the diet of life.

You cannot go within and reach the Kingdom of Heaven unless you eat the diet of life. What is this diet of life? The diet of life is healthy fruits, vegetables, seeds, nuts and grains. Healthy, meaning non-sprayed, natural, and organic produce. The diet of life includes fresh, pure water. The diet of life is life-force foods or foods cooked with the sun, slightly raw is best, if the food is compatible with being eaten raw. Eat very little cooked, processed or steamed foods.

Do not eat the dead bodies of any animal, for if you do, you will die of a disease of corruption.

Soft drinks, especially the ones containing the contaminants should be sold with a skull and cross bone on the label. You are killing yourself through drink and white sugar. Processed sugar destroys your immune system and robs your body of all nutrients and creates all vulnerabilities to disease. Take your children off of sugar and observe the peace within them. Their grades will improve because the sugar will no longer play havoc with their brain cells.

White bleached flour – a flour of death. Caffeine, another poison, should come with a warning. It also destroys the immune system.

Alcohol and all things white – white flour, white bread and white sugar – destroys brain cells. Processed sugar kills. Drugs destroy the soul and body.

Dear Sons, come back to your Mother and your Father. Step away from the diet of death.

Most worshipers of temples follow the diet of life, so we will address the synagogues of now time. We will explain to the people of the true Hebrew faith before the time of their enslavement with the Egyptians; they were pure followers of the diet of Life. They did not partake of the eating of the flesh.

Since they were under the rule of the Egyptians for so many years, they were forced to eat flesh for that was all that was available to the Hebrews. When Moses was sent to free the children of the Hebrew faith, the first of his teachings was to return the freed slaves to the diet of life.

When he returned from the mountain tops (meaning in communion with Higher Realm), he found them cooking flesh – referred to in your Bible as worshipping the golden calf.

Do you think the Egyptians would let these slaves leave with gold?

Slaves were not allowed to have gold, for they could purchase their freedom with gold. To worship the golden calf, meant that the calf was on a spit of fire, the fire set off a flame glow of gold.

When Moses returned from the Higher Consciousness to find his people had broken the laws of diet - that is referred to as him breaking the tablets – tablets meant Divine Laws. All Divine Laws were carried on stone tablets, so they would survive generations to come. His people broke the Divine Laws of diet. He could not bring them back to the Essene diet...the diet of life. So he attempted to bring them back gradually by not mixing dairy with meat and burying a knife in the hot sand was to kill bacteria. Those of you following the kosher diet and still burying a knife in the ground are misunderstanding Moses' advice. They did not have dishwashers in the deserts, so the hot sand was the only solution.

Dear Sons of Israel...let us explain what Israel means! Israel means – IS is the abbreviation for Isis – Mother. RA is an abbreviation for Ram – Father. EL is the abbreviation for God.

So when you say in your prayers 'Oh Israel, Oh Israel within me,' you are actually saying 'Oh Mother Father God, Oh Mother Father God within me.' You have mistaken the true meaning of the word Israel. How many must die, fighting over a section of Earth named Israel, when the true meaning of IS RA EL means to come unto us, your Mother and Father within?! Oh, Children of the lost interpretation, wake up!

Do you remember the prophecy that proclaimed the sacrificing of animals in your synagogues would cease when the Messiah (the Promised One) would come? Look back in time, when you stopped sacrificing animals on your alters!

He came. He taught all of you the way back to the Inner Kingdom of Heaven, but whom of you have heard His words? His teachings were Our teachings. He asked you to love God with all your heart and with all your might – this means to align with us daily and to love your neighbor as yourself.

This also means to recognize everyone as a part of the very all of Creation. There is no separation. We are all one. You have been given a visual gift of photography (Kirlian Aura photography) that shows you have a life-force in and around your body and it is even demonstrated in the plant and animal kingdom. This life-force is your true self. We are all part of this life-force.

If you see yourself as we see you, we see you as beautiful beings of our Creator, one with the very All, with a unity of Spirit. Only in the flesh do you separate and see yourself separate.

You separate by race, religion, gender, age, education, wealth and talent. You are all one of the life-force. Join us in consciousness and love.

Now, let us discuss the churches. We will start with the first church and we will tell you the whole truth.

The Roman Catholic Church...Rome did not fall, it relocated into the Roman Catholic Church. We repeat, The Roman Catholic Church.

We will take you back in time, when the Christian camps were expanding, where healings and miracles were an every day occurrence. People brought all their possessions to share with others. Unconditional love was spreading throughout the lands. Roman soldiers lay down their arms to join the camps. Remember the man whom had the greatest faith to have his servant healed without Christ having to go unto his home?

This great man led many men to the Christ camps. All that were healed spread the word. People from all lands were joining the Light of Christ. There were more than the one hundred and forty-four thousand to turn the tide of the Light and Love on Earth. The Light was winning. It was spreading like a forest fire of love and healing. All would have been healed on Earth at that time; however, the Elders of Heaven realized there were souls in the in-between worlds whom were not given the opportunity to choose the Christ Light of love and healing. The Disciples and Christians were removed from Earth to give an allowance of 2,000+ years to allow all the souls to choose the Light, but most of you have been led astray.

You have been taught under the Catholic Church that you are not allowed to go within, that you must go to a Priest as a mediator. Lies, Lies, Lies! This was created to control you. Confession is another means of control, then saying Hail Mary and Our Fathers for penance. Were you told not to recite like a parrot?

Your Bible has been tampered with during the 400 A.D.s when Mother-God was removed and again in the 1100 and 1200s from the Ecumenical and Nicene Council. Also the King James Version has been misinterpreted and tampered with.

"Go and procreate and do not spill thy seed upon thy soil." The Roman government in the form of the Roman Catholic Church chose to twist that

meaning in order to gain power and wealth. The more Catholics, the more they are able to rule.

We will explain the true meaning of go and procreate and do not spill thy seed upon thy soil. It was given to the Sons of God cohabiting with the Daughters of Man. This was a time when souls entered into lower forms of flesh on Earth, the primate form. Due to their worlds being destroyed by massive weapons, these souls were split and sought out life and found it on Earth. Earth was used as a garden for other worlds, referred to as the Blue Planet. The gods placed animals in the Garden of Eden to prevent overgrowth of the garden. The animals shared the food with the gods. When these worlds were destroyed by greed and misunderstanding of Divine Laws, it created a vacuum, you refer to them as Black Holes.

These souls whom experienced the shattering and split sought out life and ended up in the animal kingdom on Earth. The Masters of Higher Realm met with Mother Creator, your Holy Mother and I your Father, and we sent the Sons of God to cohabit with the daughters of man in order to raise the species to a higher level. It could only be the Sons of God able to do this, for having the Daughters of God cohabiting with the Sons of Man would mean our Daughters of God would carry in their wombs a lower vibration child, understand?

Birth control today or the absence of birth control is strictly the Roman Church attempting to control you, in order to fill their pockets. The Catholic Church is one of the most corrupt organizations on Mother Earth.

The Pope = The Caesar
The Cardinals = The Senate
The Priest = The Congress of Marshalls
The Bishops = The Heads of Congress and the Senate

Due to confession, the Priest took the place of the Marshall's whom kept control over Roman citizens. The Marshall's reported to the government to protect itself from being overthrown.

You may say all your repetitive prayers, they are going no where! Stop, go within and align with us and your God-selves. Return to us as our Sons.

This is my body, this is my bread. Do this in remembrance of me. We will give you our Son's true meaning of this. When you eat and drink, go within and align with your Christ-self, be in an inner level of consciousness. Be in love and peace when you eat and drink. New wine is grape juice, not alcohol.

The rest of the churches tried to break away from the darkness of the Roman Church, but they still failed to teach you the Kingdom of Heaven is with within you or how to reach us, by aligning with us within. There is not one church or synagogue or temple whom have taught you how to return to us and that you are the Sons of God.

Paul told you, but did you listen? *"Man know yourself, ye are gods."*

CHAPTER IV

Fall of Man

Man has fallen away from his God-self, his Higher Self. He is caught on the Wheel of Karma to repeat his errors for all eternity, in a maze of debt and cannot find his way out.

First, we will give you the elements man has partaken in to bring about his fall.

Man <u>ate</u> of the Tree of Knowledge of Good and Evil – the word <u>ate</u> was not recognized in your book of guidance. Man was to have dominion over the animals. You were given your guidance for your food in the Book of Genesis.

But did you understand? No, you did not.

You killed the animals you were given spiritual charge over and you ate their bodies.

Let us tell you what you have put into action on your Wheel of Karma. You have eaten dead flesh and you have taken into your cells the cell memory of the animal. This will align you with the animal kingdom.

This merging keeps man in the lower animal kingdom, grounding man's consciousness to deny him his abilities to his ascension and his alignment with his God-self. When man is grounded into the lower animal level, he is susceptible to all lower frequencies. He has killed to eat or others have killed for him to eat. You are eating death and suffering of lesser forms.

<u>Stop now</u>. <u>Cease</u>!

Stop adding to your burdens. You want life-force foods (raw, organic); foods that still contain an aura. This life-force will feed your life-force, which is part of the Creator.

When you eat animals, you will be drawn to other lower forms of diet – caffeine, processed sugars, alcohol, even drugs. It is all lower forms that keep you on the Wheel of Karma. This automatically closes the door to the Kingdom of Heaven within you and this diet of darkness will draw in lower form energies that will attach themselves to your auric shield and sometimes you physically. Yes, you will be possessed by entities of the dark. People in past times knew about possessions. You have lost the ability to recognize possessions of the dark.

You have heard the expression 'whatever possessed you to do such a thing like that?'

Most violence is done under the influence of alcohol, drugs and sugar! Yes, refined sugar is a drug!

Fathers, take your children off of sugar and see the peace and calm return to them. You will find their reasoning power has returned. Sugar breaks down the immune system. Therein lays all vulnerability to disease.

When you take a carcinogen into your physical body, your auric shield (the energy in and around your body) is depleted. It will place you in a vulnerable position to lower form entities, negative energies filled with a need to attach themselves to the weakened shield or energy force field. This will cause a personality change to the person being attached.

Why do you have so much crime and violence and murder today? Because of these dark forces attaching themselves to you and your families.

Your statistics regarding murder of women and children by their husbands and fathers are rising. If you were not punished here on Earth for your crimes, be aware your punishment will be on an even lower frequency level of life (a two-density reality). You will take on the limited, negative karma of the people/family you murdered and you have to pay this karmic debt in a lower density than Earth. Earth is a third density reality. Your acquired debts will be paid off in a more difficult, heavier density.

Woe unto you whom have killed women and children and those less strong than you and did not pay your debt on Earth. You will suffer the seeds you have sowed for eons and eons.

You were given a physical body larger and stronger to protect and support. If you went against God's laws by harming or destroying, you will pay an even longer debt of reaping. If you are one of the souls whom were not punished, you will regret not paying for your dark deeds on Earth.

Those men whom have been trained to use their bodies in law enforcement, sports and in great physical endurance and used your extra strength against women, children and the weaker, will experience a lack of physical powers for all eternity through unwellness or physical infirmity. Beware man, you were created to protect and support in pure love. The men whom abstains from carcinogens – meat, dairy, processed sugars, caffeine, tobacco, alcohol, and drugs – will be able to go within and align with us.

Every messenger from us ate the diet of life. Yes, even our Son, the Christ. He drank new wine, known as grape juice – one of the great cleansers on Earth.

"Man, know yourself, ye are gods," quote from Paul.

Come back to us while you still have time to accomplish your own inner ascension.

Go within. This is the true purpose for you to come to Earth – to choose love and ascend to your highest self.

The Wheel of Debts. You are going around and around and around, never ascending. Stop your wheel and get off!

We are in crisis with mankind's consciousness. Material values are prominent, female sexual exploitation in some countries, while there is suppression of females in other countries.

There is a rise of substance and alcohol abuse. Fast food, dead foods are the norm. Teenage murder and suicide are on the rise. Two out of three pregnant women murdered are killed by the father of their unborn child. Women's shelters are on the rise out of necessity to save the woman's life. It is not safe on the streets and country paths, for rape and murder are increasing.

Divorce is over fifty percent in some countries. Single mothers carry the weight of the world on her shoulders and some men walking away from their families and at times resenting the child support ordered by the courts. Others completely walk away. The women with children have to take on the sun energy of the absent mate, carrying his and her load. Since man has been separated from his heart and spirit chakra, he has only his red sexual chakra to survive on.

When these men make their transition, they are going to be in a lower level of existence. Their karmic debts have been added unto instead of paid for and instead of ascending to a higher level of consciousness. You men whom have harmed, hurt and even killed will carry the karmic debt of the one you have harmed for all eternity.

These souls you harmed or killed will be karma-free with the exception of their experience of victimization. The beloved souls whom have experienced such atrocities will be helped by the Angelic Realm in order to free them of the experience of being hurt, harmed, tortured, and murdered. And the doer of the misdeeds will carry the atrocities with them for eons and eons. So if someone has murdered on Earth and has not been brought to justice in your court system, their punishment will be magnified in the astral plane and in a lower dimension.

If you are saddened when the perpetrator of a crime goes free, remember what you have been taught from the Divine Laws.

"*Vengeance is mine sayeth the Lord.*"

Translated, *Vengeance is mine sayeth the Law of Karma. Or the Law of Sowing and Reaping.*

The laws of sowing and reaping – the Law of Karma is attached to your Higher Self. Everyone has a Higher Self. It is always there for you to align with.

It is your God-self that will choose to bring about your retribution if you have done harm to another. The higher evolved soul, the quicker the result of your actions will come upon you. "*God is harder on His own.*" Meaning, the higher you are evolved, the quicker your Higher Self will create the results of your actions.

The days of coming to Earth to pay off your past debts are coming to an end. You will have to go to a lower density and it will take twice as long to fulfill your past debts and be more difficult through a heavier density. Mother Earth has served, she is being given a time to rest and renew.

"Man know yourselves, ye are gods!" A quote from your Bible, but how many of you believed and if you believed, how did you act upon it? Did you go within and connect with the divine forces, so you would fulfill your divine path?

There is so much confusion on Mother Earth, since the woman's movement. Because the goddess has been suppressed and betrayed, she has to fight in sun energy, male energy in order to be treated equally. But equality is to be divinely defined.

The woman's movement hurt the feminine energy on Earth. She is now made to take on sun, male energy of child support and alimony. A man who accepts alimony and child support from a woman is giving away his power, his very reason for being on Earth. He is failing his purpose. Many women have worked to put their husband's through school, only to experience the marriage crumble. Why? Because the woman took away the power from the man by placing herself in sun energy, male energy.

Now, we hear you women cry, you want a career. You do not want to be controlled by a man. You watched your mother, grandmothers, aunts, being suppressed by a man and controlled them through their inability to work and have their own money.

We will address the working goddess in the Empowerment of Woman section of this book. We will address the wife working in accordance to the Empowerment of Man.

When you wife works, she will work in a career that is aligned with her soul. She will be free of paying the bills and debts and free of experiencing long, arduous hours. It is the man's divine purpose to love, protect and support his wife while she works in her divine choice of careers. It is not her responsibility to support and protect the family. It is your responsibility. You will learn in the Empowerment of Woman that she has come to love, nurture and spiritually inspire, while you have come to love, protect and support.

Many men – and we stress many – abused the word obey in the marriage vows. They excluded the word cherish in the vows and took the word obey and misused and misunderstood. Obey: to act in conformity with; to be at one with. The atrocities that have taken place under the misuse of the word obey have filled the Akashic Records with tears and grief.

For man to abuse and suppress the female is to abuse and suppress his own ascension. For he will ascend to the female form and have to live with the suppression and abuse that he sowed. He will become the abused female after he has ascended to the female form, for he has sown the seed of abuse and will reap the seeds of being abused.

The men whom have abandoned their families and resented child support or even failed to pay their child support, these men will experience these seeds they have sown for many lifetimes and these seeds will be sown in a lower density. It will take longer to pay off the debts owed. You have a choice to sow good seeds and care for your family by giving of yourself as a good parent and mate or experience a lower density life of suffering.

Fathers whom have killed the mothers of their unborn child have stepped away from their souls. You will take on the karmic debts of your child and its mother for all eternity. The child and mother will be karma-free with the exception of releasing the victimization from their cells of consciousness.

The Angels of the healing realm will assist the souls of victimization to release their experience, while the murderers will carry their deeds with them for eons. Beware men of violence, all you do will be done unto you!

Only men whom return unto their spirit of love will ascend, all others will relive their horrors over and over. Men return to love. Go within. Learn to serve, protect and support. Live your path. Do good works. Align with your Higher Self. Pray without ceasing, meaning align with your highest self, allow the highest forces to support you in your abilities to love, protect and support you and yours. You will be loved, protected and supported by us.

First, seek ye the Kingdom of Heaven and all other things will be added unto you. The Kingdom of Heaven is within you.

Go Within.

Chapter V

Chakras

What are they? And what is their purpose?

Chakras are energy force fields that apply to certain areas of strength to all of your bodies. You have a physical, mental, emotional, spiritual, etherical and aura body.

When your chakras are in balance and in strength, they give off health and well-being; when they are misfiring or depleted, the bodies shut down and fatigue, depression and unwellness sets in.

To keep your body's chakras healthy, eat the diet of life, drink pure water, breathe in clean, fresh air when possible, and think positive thoughts and go within to align to the unlimited Source.

The Sacred Breath is – breathe in through the nose, gently exhale through the mouth. Say silently with each breath *"Every breath I take is the sacred breath of the Creator. The Creator and I are one."* Rub your palms together, breath in the sacred breath.

Do this ten times while rubbing the palms of your hands together, then place your left palm over your third eye (the center of your forehead about three inches away from the third eye) for about twenty seconds. Rub your hands together again before you move to the next chakra. Move next to your throat chakra, approximately three inches away from the throat.

Then move to the heart, solar plexus, stomach and pelvic, hold the vision of the sacred energy balancing and energizing each chakra. Repeat with the right hand. Keep your thoughts on love and the creative energy. Allow the energy and consciousness to balance your force fields, chakras. Be good to yourself. Many healers and channels are focused on others to heal and they deplete their own force field.

Healers, stop. Heal yourselves first. Breathe in the sacred breath.

CHAPTER VI

The Valiant Ones (for Man)

Your Holy Mother and I, your Father will tell you of these Valiant souls. They come to Earth with an inner dedication to be at their highest self when needed.

Some have joined your armed services, Peace Corps, the fire department; sheriff and police departments and others have become doctors, dentists, paramedics and teachers. These souls, whom have come to Earth with an inner drive of purpose, will rise to the highest acts of kindness and bravery when called upon to do so. There is a major unlimited energy force of good and love concentrated on Earth from the celestial beings at this time and many of her children of Valiant souls from our Creator have come to Earth to do their part. These souls will leave Earth without being affected by the Wheel of Death or Karma. Sometimes the Valiant Ones will take a job of earthly pursuits, such as being in service with utilities and repairs. These souls will lend a helping hand beyond what is expected of them and they will do it with care.

Finding these souls are easy if you live in a small community, but if you live in the city, they become obscure with the consciousness of anonymity.

There is such a dichotomy on Mother Earth at this time. The Light is rising with all the enlightened souls on Earth at this time, which is now creating the darkness to attack the Light. As mankind's consciousness awakens to the Light, it creates forms of darkness that attack the Light. We are seeing this today with terrorists all over the planet.

There is a purpose for this horrific darkness and that purpose is to bring all the children on Earth together and fulfill the prophecies. There shall be one world, one belief, and one people. The brotherhood and sisterhood of man and womankind are to be built out of joining forces against the evil that is being expressed today.

Children of Earth band together against this evil. It is the purpose of the evil, to bring you to the beginning of the brotherhood and sisterhood of man and womankind. The Valiant Ones are working towards this goal to bring healing, peace and love to Mother Earth.

CHAPTER VII

Father God's Divine Laws for Manhood

First, you must recognize the purpose of your visit to Mother Earth. You are given a chance to enter into the land of nod, referred to in the book of Genesis. You have heard the expression 'to nod off' in reference to going to sleep. You are given the gift of starting a new life without your old lives influencing you. It is to give you a new opportunity to rise to the highest of yourself, to choose love, service to others, kindness and wisdom.

Just before you are allowed to come back to Mother Earth, you must sit with your past triumphs and failures. You will sit before Kumad, the Master of the Akashic Records. You sit at the feet of all the Masters and you are given a choice and choose a particular life mission assignment.

Some of you try to compensate for past misdeeds, so you may choose heavy burdens to overcome. Some choose dysfunctional parents to learn from, as what not to do in parenting.

Others are born into poverty and choose to overcome the limitation of poverty. Some choose to be born into great wealth with the intention of using the wealth for the good of others.

Some choose a limited physical body in order to overcome and to inspire others. There is the choice of racial challenges in order to overcome prejudices. Some choose a religion to experience what was not experienced in a past life. The souls whom have hurt others in past lives will choose the sect of people he hurt in a past life and become one of them. If a soul had a slave and abused the slave, then he will choose one form or another to be enslaved.

Whatever you have sown, so shall you reap.

You will also be given the opportunity to heal a relationship from a past experience by being a parent to one you have harmed or they have harmed you.

Be careful you do not judge your fellow man in his choices of challenges. You may be judging a Master Soul whom came to Earth to give others an opportunity to give unto him.

Judge ye not!!!

The most important Divine Law is to love the Creator, your Holy Mother and I, your Holy Father and your Higher Self with all your heart and soul.

To break this law is to deny us within you. Separating from your divine self results in hatred, judgment, jealousy, anger and looking to earthly gods such as man's ego (you see yourself as greater or lesser than others), money, jobs, alcohol, drugs, tobacco, sexual intimacy (sex without love), eating flesh, processed sugar, caffeine, white flour.

To fulfill the first Commandment means to clearly spiritually align with us at all times. *"To pray without ceasing,"* as Paul said.

This is done by going within and allowing us to be with you in consciousness. We will carry you through every moment of your life. In the connection, you will feel a presence of peace within you. And you will realize you are connected to all living matter, so you will be at one with all life. It will remove you from judgment, which will remove you from errors of thought to prevent you from paying penitence in the future. As this energy flows through you, you will become more empowered, more inspired, more creative for the energy flow comes from the Creator and the Creator can only create and love only creates.

To hate, to hurt, to kill is to walk away from the Creator and become and uncreator! You are hating yourself when you hate others. They are part of the whole of the Creator's energy.

To hurt another is to send that hurt out into the ethers and it will return unto you ten-fold.

To destroy or kill is to take that soul's journey and end their journey. You will have to take on their journey and/or mission in other karmic incarnations. Their karma is now your karma. If you choose to fulfill your divine mission here on Earth these laws will apply:

1. You will divinely align.
2. You will share that divine alignment with others.
3. You will strive to be the best of yourself; with our support all things are possible.
4. You will protect all females and children placed upon your path of life.
5. You will support the females and children in your family.
6. You will protect and support those in need within your reach.

If you are a man on Earth that has accomplished these six tasks for your lifetime, then you will ascend to a higher dimension of expressions – *"My Father's house has many mansions."*

When you pass onto the next dimension, you will pass onto the level of your consciousness. If you are content and joyous on Earth, you will create that very same reality on the etherical level. You take your reality with you. However, if you are troubled, worried, anxious, you will carry this consciousness with you too. If you have done evil, you will be drawn to the lower levels of expression.

Now, let us discuss the limitations of man's creation of religion. Religious beliefs are just that a belief that is practiced, religiously.

Have you not be warned about parroting your words to us?

Your words must come from your heart and soul and in your moment. We do not want any prepared speeches. We respond to alignment to us and a merging with us that fills your temple, body with our presence. This presence is beyond Earth density. You are bringing unto you the very essence of Creation. Out of the essence it will transform your earthy experience into a heavenly one. You will create, love, overcome obstacles, and heal relationships, bodies, minds and spirits.

First, seek ye the Kingdom of Heaven and all other things will added unto you!!! This means go within and align with us. Allow us to fill you.

You are not alone in protecting and supporting your family. We will supply the source of strength within that will not only carry you, but will give you the wisdom to choose correctly.

The Kingdom of Heaven is within you.

You ask 'how do I go within?' We will show you. First, place all outside interference on hold. Turn off all your ringers on your telephones.

Place yourself in a comfortable position. Feet flat on the floor. Close your eyes; breathe deeply, but gently. Silently affirm 'I am. I am.' several times until you feel a peace within your whole body.

When you feel connected, you will feel a slight lightness in your body. Focus your inner vision in the middle of your inner forehead. Ask your questions, silently. Then wait patiently for the answer. The answer will come.

If you have a yes or no question, take a deep breath, ask yeah or nay. One question at a time. Then pay attention to your solar plexus. If your solar plexus is peaceful that is a yes. If not, that is a no. Be patient with yourselves. We are within you, waiting for you. All you have to do is go within.

As you go within for guidance, for your divine right career, know that we will guide you and support you in all your endeavors.

Be cautious of what you think. Keep your thoughts on a positive level, especially what thought or words you place after 'I am.'

Examples of negative thoughts:

I am tired.

I am bored.

I am angry.

I am sick.

Examples of positive thoughts:

I am. I am.

I am happy.

I am patient.

I am loved.

I am peaceful.

I am healthy.

I am wise.

I am wealthy.

We will cover all religions now. If your religion teaches you to go within, you are close. We have sent you our messengers and you have created religions out of them.

We sent you Christ with his message of love, to forgive your enemies. You created many Christian Churches.

We sent you Buddha, you chant repeatedly.

We sent you Mohammed, whom taught you to love and forgive. Those of you whom stand behind one of our messengers and torture and kill will suffer such great darkness of spirit.

You worshipped them instead of applying their teachings to your life. All our messengers taught love above all else. To love your Holy Mother and I, means to align with us. To love your neighbor as yourself is to recognize the same energy in them as within you.

Take a moment, feel our presence within you. Now, recognize the same presence within your neighbor. Now, take that recognition and share it with an enemy. Bless your enemy with love. Feel the unlimited love pour through your enemy; next allow that love to pour over all the children of Earth. Feel Mother Earth being filled with unconditional love.

These misguided souls whom feel they have to kill or murder will be shocked to find that all the souls they have murdered will be free of the Wheel of Karma.

They will only have to clear their victimization beliefs and the murderers will carry their karma for all eternity.

Judge ye not, let ye be judged likewise. You whom have killed will carry your victim's karmic debts and those debts will be carried out in a much lower density than Earth. Earth is a third density reality or illusion, which ever you prefer to name it. You will be sent to a two-dimensional illusion and you will carry your karma and all those you have harmed upon your soul.

All there is is love. All other is a separation from love.

You were told in the very first Chapter of your Bible that God is Love. Hate is a separation from love, a separation from us. You have free will. You may either choose love or you may separate yourself from love. It is your choice. If you choose love, all the blessings of the unlimited Source will be yours. *"First seek ye the Kingdom of Heaven and all other things will be added unto you."*

If you seek a separation from love you will experience the struggle of the separation from your unlimited inner power.

Religions are limited by their rules and regulations. Once in a great while one of you will reach us or the Holy Spirit through prayer, but if you are too busy with the limited rules of your religion, how can you practice the unlimited consciousness? You cannot serve two masters.

When you try to worship through the limited eyes of your church, temple or synagogue, even though a messenger came before you with the truth, did you follow their message?

No, most of you made a religion out of the messenger and did lip service to us. Your prayers must come from the deep well within you. We are not outside of you!

The Roman Catholic Church – Rome did not fall; it just relocated into the Roman Catholic Church. We will take you back in time when our Son came in this last incarnation to bring the truth of love to the world. Because there was such love on Earth at that time, Christ did not come alone. We sent millions of messengers with Him at that time to bring the children of man back to being the children of God.

The Holy Spirit worked with all our messengers so much so that the Roman Army was lying down their swords and becoming one with the love and Light. Men and women were coming from all over the lands to seek the Christ. Christ traveled many lands and over many oceans to bring the truth of love and wisdom to the world. There was a turbulence of love, healing transformation on Earth SO GREAT that eventually all would align with the highest of consciousness

But! Because there were so many souls on the etherical side of Earth it was decided to withdraw the Light and allow over two thousand years for man and womankind an opportunity to return to Love. Now your extra time allotted to choose love is coming to an end.

Mother Earth needs to be replenished. You will have to choose love in either a lower or higher density depending on your ability to love or inability to love.

Those experiencing an inability to love will be drawn to a lower density. Those whom have expressed love will ascend to a higher level of expression.

While you still have time on Mother Earth, please remember; every good deed and thought on Earth is worth a hundred thousand good deeds in Spirit form.

Man, know yourself, ye are gods.

Start to behave as if you are!

Love, protect, support and most of all align with us at all times. To pray without ceasing means to be connected to us and Higher Realm, an awareness so to speak at all times, be our Sons. Come from love and love will support and protect you.

Man has lost his way. He has disconnected to his Spirit. His base chakra is separated from his heart chakra. There is a dark murky band between the red chakra and the orange chakra that blocks off man's sexual desires to his emotions, heart and spirit.

This block can appear at an early age, where the young man's affections were criticized or rejected so he started to withdraw. Restrictions placed upon him would train him to keep his emotions in check. 'A stiff upper lip' or 'tough it out' he has been told. 'Only girls cry,' etc.

Add this to drugs, alcohol and fast food without life-force energy in the food, movies with sexual exploitation and violence. Man is in danger of falling further from his true self, his God-self. *"Man, know yourself, ye are Gods,"* said Paul.

I, your Holy Father and your Holy Mother, will share with you the Divine Laws to manhood, or in truth, the Divine Laws to your God-self. We are reaching out to you through this channel to bring you back home to us.

For most of you, when you come to Mother Earth, you are descending to a lower or similar level of consciousness. First, we must address the purpose for your journey to Earth.

The reason you choose to come to Earth is because for every good deed you perform on Earth in the third density is worth one hundred thousand good deeds on the astral density.

Why do you wish to accomplish a good deed?

The greater the love you express, the highest you ascend in consciousness.

The higher you ascend in love, the greater the capacity to experience love and creativity and an expansion of the presence of your divine self. Love is the essence of creativity. To love, to create, to give, to grow is the purpose of the soul, to return to the Creator in unlimited unconditional love, which is euphoria beyond comprehension on the physical plane of Earth.

Before you are allowed on Earth, you must sit through a screening of past deeds or misdeeds. Then you will be allowed to choose a circumstance of birth that will give you an opportunity to accomplish the healing of past deeds or fulfill a mission or journey.

At this time there are numerous souls, too numerous to count for your understanding, whom have come to Earth without any limited, negative karma attached to their souls. These souls come from many elevated consciousness that are not attached to the Akashic Records. They are here as healers, mystics, the clearers of the Akashic Records, musicians, artists, scientists of healing, natural health teachers, chiropractors, acupuncturists, healing acupressure, herbalists, writers, inventors bringing healing to Earth. These souls have come to heal the Earth and her children.

These are souls whom have entered into a forgetful state and had to wake up to their true identity. We will address the volunteer souls in *Are You a Lightworker?*

You are given the gift of life when you come to Earth and with this gift your past cell life memory is removed in order for you to be given a fresh start.

You will have memory of your past life cell memory, which will appear as phobias or fears, favorite foods or countries or anything you have a natural aversion to, such as fear of the dark, enclosed places, great heights, etc, allergies to certain foods. This is all cell memory from negative, limited past life experience.

Now we will address your purpose on Earth – you coming to Earth as a male form.

You are to love, protect and support all the females and children in your sphere. When in public, see to the comfort and safety of women and children, open doors; give up your seat on public transportation and see to their safety against any harm.

CHAPTER VIII

Sins of the Father Fall upon the Son (for Man)

"*The sins of the father fall upon the son,*" a quote from the Bible that translates to: the programming of the parents is passed down to their children.

This truth is overlooked or it is also greatly misunderstood. Your Holy Mother and I, your true Father, will explain this to you. Our purpose in doing so is to free you from all earthy limitations and addictions.

First, your soul will be drawn to the parents you are assigned to. This is to work out the past debts the parents and child may have to complete. Then the child will be programmed from the womb regarding the father and mother's consciousness during the pregnancy. This consciousness or programming will be passed on to the child. If the pregnancy was not planned or the child unwanted, the infant will be imprinted with that consciousness as well. This is why many adopted children have a feeling of not being loved from the very beginning. They will sometimes seek out their birth mother or father to resolve this unwanted programming. Most times they end up disappointed.

There are also the limited, negative patterns the parents have received from their parents, so the child must overcome all these limited, negative programs. To overcome this programming, you do so by releasing these negative patterns and returning to us, your true parents – Mother-Father God.

Your Holy Mother and I, your Father wish to address addictions of relationships. If you are in an addictive relationship with a toxic mate, you need to return in your mind's eye to your parent's behavior and patterns. *"The sins of the father fall upon the son."*

The patterns, be they negative or positive are imprinted upon you. If your mate is toxic and you feel compelled to stay in the dysfunctional relationship, then you are playing out your parent's patterns. It has nothing to do with love. It is reliving negative patterns of your parents in your life. Your feeling of love is a compulsion to relive your parent's patterns.

Go back in time and release the negative patterns. See yourself blessing your parents with God's healing Light. Pour it over your parents, and then pour it over you. Fill yourself with our divine love. Trust you are worthy of a love – a pure love.

Fill your heart and body with our love. We will repair your belief system into ascending to a higher level of consciousness by blessing, releasing and erasing the limited, negative programming you have received from your parents.

You are worthy of a divine love, heaven sent.

Know you are enough.

You are whole, total and complete. The Kingdom of Heaven is within you.

CHAPTER IX

The Dark (for Man)

The dark is only the absence of Light. The gods of dark came into existence when they became restless of being the Gods of Light, the Sons of God. These gods turned their consciousness away from the Light. The further away from the Light, the darker the gods of dark became. These gods played their games in the astral realm until they took their game to lower realms. The results were greed, corruption, murder, mayhem, wars, and atrocities, ending and destroying many levels of consciousness and other worlds. These worlds were obliterated, creating black holes in the Universe.

The gods of dark's games are coming to an end. The Light has gathered together in order to end the dark's influence on Mother Earth and the eternal Universe.

These gods have created so much misery and havoc. Their sowings will now close in on them. They will have to answer to the heavens. The laws of karma will end the gods of dark's game sooner than anyone knows or will even realize. For our Son of Light and Love made a promise to the children of Earth – He will return and walk the Earth for over a thousand years. There shall be peace on Earth and good will towards men.

Now, we will tell you how you can free yourselves and your family from the control and corruption of the dark to help bring the peace on Earth and good will towards men, as prophesized by our Son.

We will show you how you may end the gods of dark's control. The gods of dark control man and womankind's consciousness through eating of the Tree of Knowledge of Good and Evil. You were told this in your very first book – Genesis.

Even though your Bible has been tampered with, the sentence is still intact. Adam and Eve were thrown out of the Garden of Eden because they ate of the Tree of Knowledge of Good and Evil. The operative word being ate!

Very few children of Earth have realized the in-depth meaning of this statement. We will give you all the levels of control that the gods of dark use for their control and their games. These next pages will be devoted to freeing mankind from the control of the dark – your diet – what you eat, drink and take into your body can be filled with the energy of the Creator or the lack of energy, meaning dead flesh (meat), dairy, alcohol, sugar, drugs, cigarettes, chewing tobacco, caffeine, and bleached flour. All these things are attached to the dark (the gods of dark). When you eat a carcinogen, it places a crack in your auric shield. This allows the attachment to enter your shield and feed off your body and mind.

These attachments are black reptilian, vine-like attachments – lower forms of evil that attach and feed off of you, controlling you and keeping you addicted. All humans addicted to carcinogens are being controlled by the dark.

We observe our children fighting these addictions. We see these lower form attachments strangling some of you. These attachments cause personality changes.

The most destructive addiction causing element you are feeding to your children is sugar. Parents STOP giving your children sugar. It is filled with bleach. It places a crack in your children's auric shield and they become agitated and hyperactive. Sugar addiction leads to alcohol and drug addiction.

Give them all organic, non-heated honey, pure maple syrup, agave, xylitol, barley and rice syrup in small amounts. Let them enjoy fruit as their sweetener. Please protect your children from the dark!

Every drag off a cigarette allows the dark into your lungs, nose cavity, skin, hair, eyes, even your third eye. The creatures that follow the dark are of the lowest form of consciousness and you are inviting them into your body! Think about it.

Meat! You are eating a dead body of a murdered animal. Thou shall not kill!! When you eat dead flesh, the dark entities that feed off the dead will enter your body with the killed animal. Beware this is the dark at its very best – a sales pitch – steaks, hamburgers, drumsticks, and roasts are all camouflage for dead, murdered animals.

Alcohol has sometimes been referred to as spirits, coming from the dark spirits whom would be drawn to the alcohol. Have you not witnessed a personality change in a person under the influence of alcohol?!

You have the power to do your part in ending the game of dark on Earth. Drink pure water; eat organic fruits, vegetables, seeds, nuts and grains.

Walk away from all carcinogens:

1. Alcohol
2. Sugar
3. Tobacco
4. Meat
5. Dairy (animal)
6. Drugs
7. Deep-fried foods

Go within and align with us, your Holy Parents. If drugs are required for a much needed operation find the least offensive one to you. Then after your surgery, cleanse your body through diet and prayer. Eventually, you will have non-evasive surgery, so drugs will no longer be needed.

Pray when going into surgery. Ask God, the Light and Angels to surround you for protection. Let go of all anger. Anger is a tool of the dark. The gods of dark celebrate in your anger. To express anger is to say you are separate from your good, your God or love – are all one and the same.

Be at peace and know the Light has dominion over the dark. Join the children of Light now. End the game of dark. Bring love, peace, forgiveness, and healing to Mother Earth and all her children. It only takes one hundred and forty-four thousand to turn the tide. Have you have asked yourself 'What may I do?'

This we ask of you. Turn to us, your Holy Mother and Father; we are awaiting your return.

CHAPTER X

Prophecies for the Future

During the holidays, the winter solstice, all of you should be doing less activity – do pampering things, self-nurturing, healing teas and soups, saunas, massages, body cleansings, resting and nurturing, instead of celebrating the holidays by the control of the dark with sugar, meat, dairy, and alcohol.

This conspiracy was created by the dark in the time of Rome and laid out to weaken the child of God instead of renewing and strengthening them, making them vulnerable, at the mercy to the control of the dark by celebrating in the middle of the winter solstice.

We are going to give you a visual picture of what the future will look like – your work day will be no longer than 4-hours a day, 6 at the very most, over 80 percent of the workforce will work out of their homes, and a major shift in the workforce will work for pleasure instead of monetary gain, resulting in more abundance for them personally. For where you love, you will be abundant. The film and food industry will do 4-hour shifts. Travel will be cut down to a bare minimum and life-force foods will grow at your fingertips in your home.

There will be scientific machines brought to Mother Earth that will align with acupuncture points and release blockages within your bodies. This will bring in your balanced Chi and align you so you can meditate correctly and you will feel renewed. It will be a common occurrence to wake up in the morning after your body eliminating from the day before, you merging and aligning with us, Mother-Father God and Higher Realm. We will communicate with you as to what this day shall hold. Be prepared for spiritual creativity and alignment to reign throughout your day, both work and play.

We, in the Heavens (Higher Realm), celebrate play, joy and euphoria every day. The children on Earth have felt this compelling energy to accomplish success; however they have been misdirected in these accomplishments. Before you come to Earth, you realize you may accomplish more on Earth than in the heavens (astral plane), for one good deed on Earth is worth one hundred thousand on the astral or heavenly planes. As you come to Earth and go into the land of nod, your cell memory is not quite clear, so you have a sense of urgency to accomplish, complete, and do. However, all we have asked for all of you to remember is to love God with all your heart and mind, love one another, and to serve man and womankind. While many of you are running around accruing wealth, world recognition (fame), properties, automobiles and mechanical toys, the real purpose for you to come to Earth is to love – this is recognizing the spirit in all life forms on Earth, including yourselves.

Choose God and Love over judgment, bigotry, hatred and separation. Choose unity, spirit recognition, the brotherhood and sisterhood of man and womankind and serve one another with a joyful heart. Return Mother Earth to her healthy, loving state, you originally found her.

Your Holy Parents, Mother-Father God.

Introduction to Empowerment of Woman

I must admit as a channel, I have had more communications from Father God, but now this is to change, for Mother-God will dictate the Divine Laws of womanhood. Womans! Notice that woman is two letters added to man. These letters were abbreviated for womb. The womb of man. The womb is the divine receiver of mankind consciousness. This means that woman is only in her power when she is in her divine receivership of the unlimited Source. All women have to do, in consciousness, is to stand still and receive her unlimited Source. She is the receiver of her good.

There are duplicate chapters in both sections of this book (Empowerment of Woman and Empowerment of Man) because the information applies to both women and men. The duplicate chapters are: The Valiant Ones, The Sins of the Father Fall upon the Son, The Dark, and Prophecies for the Future.

Chapter XI

The Divine Laws of Woman

Woman's role or mission is: To love, nurture and align and show the way to align with Higher Realm for her and her loved ones. In other words, be the spiritual guide to the divine Source within all of you, within her family and surrounding family. She is the nurturer of her family.

We will return you to the book of Genesis to explain its true meaning. The book of Genesis is written in parables and symbols. The word Adam means atom of God. The word Eve means Mother Nature.

The atom of God entered into the form of flesh on Earth – Mother Nature. The story of taking the rib from man means that woman is the polarity of man. Man is the co-creator with God. And woman is the divine receiver from God. Women, you are only in your divine power, when you align with your divinity and all your good will come unto you. The Kingdom of Heaven is within you!

Let us discuss this apple. If Eve had given Adam an apple, we would have been very pleased. They ate of the Tree of Knowledge of Good and Evil. They did not follow their guide of eating seeds, nuts, fruits, vegetables and gains. They ate the animals that they were to have dominion over. To have dominion over, is to love and care for.

Stop right now, all of you whom have pets or have had pets as children. Stop and think about killing that pet and eating it as a roast or hamburger. Now, do you see the abomination you participate in every time you eat steak, chicken, fish, burgers, sushi, roast lamb, pork, cat, or dog? You have eaten dead bodies of the animal kingdom that you were given dominion over. You will take on their consciousness, Beloved Ones.

This is the reason you stay on the Wheel of Karma or the Wheel of Death. The last enemy to be overcome is death – when the Lion shall lay down with the Lamb. All will be aligned with the diet of life.

Women, you are responsible for the nurturing of the family. You prepare the food for your family. If your family's tastes are ingrained in the flavor of meat, there are many vegetarian meat replacements. Vegetarian gravies, roasts, burgers, vegetarian chicken, even vegetarian fish has been reproduced to fill those acquired tastes. If you find a product that is unpalatable, try another or ask at your natural food store for advice.

The woman is to be cherished by her mate, husband. If you are not cherished, you are in a diminished relationship. If you are in a diminished relationship, you are dishonoring your God-self – your goddess energy.

Honor yourself by only allowing yourself to love and be loved in the presence of your God-self.

Honor thy Father and thy Mother means to align with us, Dear Ones. Then you will be comforted in our energy and consciousness. You will be guided to the divine right love in a mate. You will be given direction and guidance in your choice of careers and vocations. You will feel the presence within you. This presence will be filled with peace and wisdom – a peace that surpasses all understanding. When you align with us, we will guide you in all your endeavors.

As a child, you have chosen parents of Earth whom will fulfill your choices of past debts. All of you will differ in experience. Some of you will choose loving parents and others will have brutal physical abuse experiences.

Go within; allow us to heal your wounds. Use your wounds to discover what you came to heal on Mother Earth. Maybe you came to learn how to heal wounds from your childhood to help others to heal their wounds. There will be a purpose for the suffering. Go within Dear Ones and find the purpose of your experience and find your true purpose and divine mission on Earth. Honor the Father and the Mother within you.

You have a force field in and around you. This force field (aura) must be cared for, through pure life-force foods and water, complete alignment with the life-force within you, because it is the mission for the woman to nurture. Give yourself the support you require to be the nurturer. If you are a single mother without support, then go within. Align with us, we will support you. Purchase organic fruits and vegetables. If you work long hours, buy the vegetables already cut up.

Leave fresh fruit and seeds and nuts out for the children to snack on. One day have vegetables cut with a dip for a snack, the next day, a bowl of seeds, another day, fruit, nuts, etc.

Allow your children to eat snacks that will heal and be filled with nutrition. Allow your children a good healthy diet, which will transform energy in your family, bring peace and raise grade point averages.

The poisons to children are processed sugars, diary (animal milk, cheese, ice cream, etc.), meat and caffeine. Sugar leads to addictions – drugs and alcohol. Mothers take back your power and end the cycle of addiction. Free your children from the Wheel of Death and end disease in your family and in your lifetime. You have the power – use it.

Instead of packing your children in the car after struggling to get them in their Sunday Best and going to a church; sit down quietly with your children and teach them that the Kingdom of Heaven is within them and that your Holy Father and I, your Holy Mother are their true parents and that we will be here for all eternity. We will love, nurture and care for all of you. Go within, teach your children to go within. Be a family connected to the unlimited force within all of you. Come home to us, Dear Ones.

If you are filled with our love, you will be able to show that love to your family.

CHAPTER XII

The Out-of-Balance Female

The female whom feels she must be aggressive in order to succeed in life has taken on sun energy or male energy. The out-of-balance female will offend without knowing why she is offending. She may follow professions that are dominated by males, but she will be in her true power when she stays in her female goddess, moon energy.

While in moon energy, she will speak her truth and practice her profession, while connected to her inner core of the unlimited Source. She will divinely align and find a divine flow of energy supporting her. She will discover after she practices this divine connection that it will carry throughout her work day and profession.

We will talk of the feminine energy so you will understand its true meaning. It is the female who receives the sperm and the sperm activates the egg, out of the polarity energy of giving and receiving. The female creates life – creation just out of receiving. This is the truth that must be understood fully. All you have to do, as a female, is receive. This is not only your right; it is the Divine Laws of femininity of being a female. Women stand still and know you are the divine receivers of your good. Go within and align with us and your Higher Self. You will draw unto you your guidance and good. The Great Void, the Creator, the very all is feminine energy. It is the consciousness of receiving and in that receiving creation is created. Women, you are in your divine power by going within and aligning to the unlimited Source that is available to you.

Love – now let us discuss this very misunderstood word – love. Many think it is a personal feeling of possession. No, it is not. Love is an alignment with the highest Source available to you and the recognition of the life-force within every living thing you come in contact with and that recognition, love will spread and you will experience an expanded reality of unconditional love. Recognition of the life-force is to recognize and align with the unlimited power. To align with the unlimited power is to be present with Creation. To be present with Creation is to be one with the very all. To be one with the very all is to be in the presence of your God-self.

Paul said, *"Man/woman, know yourselves, ye are gods."*

Go within and align with us. Take that alignment and share it with your family or just yourself if you do not have a family. When a hundred and forty-four thousand souls go within and align with your Holy Father and I, your Mother, in that alignment, you will recognize the life-force in all living matter, and the brother and sisterhood of man and womankind will manifest and the Christ will walk the planet for a thousand years. The prophecies will be fulfilled. Peace on Earth, good will towards man and woman and the Lion shall lay down with the Lamb.

Women, we must speak to you as the nurturers. If you are in a relationship that does not honor you or cherish you and your children are being abused, go within, call on us, we will guide you out of the darkness to find the path out of the hell you have manifested.

Get you and your children out of harm's way. There are authorities and shelters now available. In your trauma, you may feel separate from us, but find a peaceful place and make sure you are out of harm's way, then go within and we, your Holy Parents, will be there for you.

You are made in our image. That means you are precious to us and worthy of pure love and kindness. You are the child of God. We do not create victims. Victims belong to the dark. If your mate is abusive, drinks or takes drugs, get out now with the protection of the authorities.

The dark is fighting its last effort to win this planet and her children, but the Light is winning. Do not support the dark by enabling the addiction. Walk away, turn the other cheek. To turn the other cheek means to turn away from the problem or the dark. Make sure you are first safe. Find the authorities, press charges against the abuser, for if he does not pay his debt to you and society on Earth, he will suffer in a lower existence, in a two-dimensional reality. Your abuser will be given a weak body and an abusive mate to abuse them for eons and eons.

For the men, husbands and mates whom have hurt, maimed or killed women and children, they will regret not paying their debt on Earth for they will not be allowed back on Earth and their suffering will be more magnified in the lower dimension. Woe, unto you men whom have been given strength and power and misused this strength and power against women and children. Woe unto you.

The man is the protector and provider. The woman is the protected and in turn, she is the nurturer. She is to nurture her husband and family and provide a base for peace, love and well-being, praise, encouragement, and spiritual awareness. The divine awareness that is within all of you, this is the part of the partnership the woman is responsible for, but if the man is not protecting and supporting, the family structure falls apart.

In the marriage vows you take, it says those whom God (good, love) have joined together, let not man put asunder. If your mate is not bringing love or his or her soul's mission to the marriage, then the marriage is a false one.

Do you think we are pleased when you stay married and break your vows? You are living a lie.

You stay together because of the children or money or your religion or habit. This is another abomination to your Holy Father and I, Your Mother. If you are not aligning with us, as a couple and family and are not loving, cherishing, sharing, supporting and nurturing in your marriage, you have a false marriage. You are living a lie. You are breaking the Divine Laws of marriage. You do not have a marriage, you have an empty vessel, an empty shell – you are mocking God, love and Creation!

Religious, means to do a task religiously, to repeat a ceremony over and over.

Some of you reach us in spite of this method. Did not our Son warn you not to parrot prayers? Did He not ask of you to forgive seventy times seventy?

How many times have you been asked to judge not? Over four hundred times in your Bible!

But we hear your judgment. Your repeating of the same prayers goes no where! You place ash on your foreheads, why? What does this accomplish?

The kindness you express to others in secret is more acceptable to us than these outer world shows.

Go within and align with us. We will lift your Spirit to the Heavens within you. Accept the life-force within all. The life-force within all living beings is our beloved Creator and the Creator is in all life.

There are boundaries only in the minds of limitation. What does religion do? It separates the Protestants from the Catholics, Catholics from the Hebrews, the Hebrews from the Muslims, the Muslims from the Seiks, and the Seiks from the Curds, etc., etc.

How many have hated or killed for religion? How many must die for the separateness of religion?

If you are expressing anger, judgment and violence through your misguided view of your religion, Dear Ones, you are creating a belief in separateness from God, good, love for your eternity. Unless you turn back to your Creator, Mother-Father God and your own divinity, you will experience the separateness of your soul being parted from the divine Kingdom of Heaven within you.

No true follower of our messengers would advocate anger, hate or violence. These messengers would tell you it would damn your soul to suffering for eons and eons. These misguided souls whom maim, hurt and kill for an idea of hate have not only created a reality of darkness for themselves, they will have to take on the karma of the souls they killed. And if any of the souls of the killed were our volunteers from other dimensions, souls without karma, then their soul has interfered with the divine conspiracy upon this planet. To interfere with the divine conspiracy is to tempt the dark to the nth degree. When you go to the bottom of the darkest well, you will drink the greatest of our sorrows. It is a Divine Law. Nations, religions, go within, join in sharing love and respect of each other. It is now time for the prophecies to be fulfilled. One nation under God, one bank, one church, one people.

The new Heaven and new Earth are within all of you. Go within, Dear Ones. The Kingdom of Heaven is within you. So many of you Dear Ones wear your religion like a shield. You stay in the limitation of your beliefs, spout your ideas of us and close your minds to the unlimited Spirit within you. You cannot place the Creator into a small belief system. She is infinite, unlimited, never ending, beyond measure. Take away your limited beliefs and go within, find us, Dear Ones, and join the unlimited Source.

Take stock in your patterns of thought. Are you filling your mind with loving thoughts or are you re-thinking and re-talking the trauma or frustration you experienced that day or even that week? If you are reliving unpleasantness, you are recreating the idea of stress, frustration and suffering. You are bringing the negative into your new positive day. Place your focus on your inner connection with your unlimited Spirit and observe the unlimited Spirit fill you to capacity, transforming your day. You have the power, go within, soon!

Focus on thoughts you want to manifest in your life. For example – give thanks for inner and outer peace when you are experiencing chaos. Give thanks for perfect health when you are challenged in the health area. Give thanks for perfect love, perfect wisdom, or divine love, peace, health and wisdom. It is based on a Divine Law, Dear Ones.

Ask and believe it has been given unto you. When someone gives you a gift you say thank you. Use this technique of gratitude by thanking your Holy Parents for divine guidance and all your divine blessings. Go within and feel the unlimited presence within you. Allow this presence to fill you and then let it spill over and fill the room. Share this fulfillment with your loved ones.

When mommies have to be daddy's too! Two! So many mothers are carrying a double load with single parenting. Most of them feel overwhelmed and if they are attempting to be a single parent without the inner guidance, they will experience a sense of hopelessness. Single moms, Dearest Ones, in your Holy Father's and I, your Holy Mother, turn to us, we will support you.

Teach your children to go within, share our presence with your children and then watch the peace fill your lives; answers and support will come. Go within. Single moms, go within. *"First seek ye the Kingdom of Heaven within you and all other things shall be added unto you."*

We are here to support you to lighten your burdens. Ask and it shall be given unto you. Seek and ye shall find. Knock and the door will be opened unto you. It is our promise.

Woe, unto you fathers, whom have left the full burden of your children on the shoulders of the Goddess. Men that abandon their children to the Goddess and leave the burden upon her shoulders will spend many lifetimes reliving the burden upon their shoulders that they left to the Goddess. These lifetimes will not be allowed on Earth. These men will go to a lower dimension to experience these burdens with more travail. Only by loving and serving will your soul grow.

Why would you wish for your soul to grow? This is the reason you come to Earth. You stood before the Council of Light to give yourself the opportunity to have your memory erased and come to Earth with a clean slate, so to speak. You are to align with the Kingdom of Heaven within and choose love and service. This illuminates your soul to a higher frequency, and then you become more enlightened and free yourself from the Wheel of Death or Karma.

Many will return to the Council of Light and realize they have failed. They have lowered the frequency of their soul by living a selfish and decadent life. Dear Ones, if your life is empty, go within and we will guide you.

CHAPTER XIII

Prayer

Prayer! Yes, prayer changes things, but you must know how to pray.

"Ask and believe it has been given unto you!"

"Pray without ceasing."

"What ever a man or woman thinks of themselves, so are the man or woman."

These are the keys our Son Jesus and his disciple Paul gave you.

To pray without ceasing means to stay in the consciousness of inner connectedness with the Kingdom of Heaven within you at all times.

To ask and believe it has been given unto you, in an inner knowingness from your inner connectedness with the Kingdom of Heaven within you and that connectedness will always supply your needs. When you are connected to your Inner Kingdom, you know you are a child of God. When you truly know you are Our child, you will know all is well, peaceful, healthy and abundant.

The truth shall set you free. Go within, become Our children. We are waiting for you, Dear Ones. To align, love and nurture, this is a woman's journey. She must learn to stand still in consciousness and receive from the unlimited Source. This can be a difficult task when most action carried out by others is male action energy.

To be a woman is to be an advanced soul. She has lived as a man in past existences and ascended to a female soul. A female soul is closer to the Creator, for the Creator is feminine. Yes, Dear Ones, the Creator is feminine!

The gods of dark and some religious doctrines would have you believe otherwise. It is all the female species whom bring forth life from their bodies.

The gods of dark started playing a game before Earth's time, and then they brought their game to Earth. The game was to separate from the Creator and the dark created this game of good versus evil.

The only game they could create was to separate from good, God, love, Light! This game has been played for over seven million Earth years. Now, it is coming to an end. The gods of dark are reaching you through ideas and diet. Let me explain, Dear Ones.

The idea of separation is the main idea of the gods of dark. To be separate from the Creator or your Holy Father and I, your Mother is their most important part of their game. To keep their game going, they will support separatism – prejudices, anger and hatred. They will do this through earthly belief systems, such as groups, religious or non-religious, through the idea of separatism, through diet, drugs, carcinogens, sexual exploitation diminishing the female and making her an object to sexual stimulation without love. Again, the separatism of the divine Goddess is an abomination to the Creator.

The female is to be honored, cherished, and valued. NOT degraded, separated by her body parts.

Prayer and alignment! This is where your power lies. You will fill yourselves with the power and it will spill out of you to share with others. This is an energy of unconditional love. It is not an idea of Allah, God, Buddha, Christ or the Lord. We hear you verbalizing – Allah said this, Buddha said that, God said this, the Lord said this! Stop with the Saids!

Stop wearing our variations of names like a verbal banner. It gets you absolutely no where. If anything, it is an offence. You gain nothing by the mentalization of the idea of love. You will empower yourselves by going within and filling yourselves with love, light, peace, wisdom and the healing energy that is attached to the Kingdom of Heaven within you.

It is a silent experience. It is not for the clattering of voices. *"Whom worships me in secret shall be rewarded openly."* Out of your connection with us, you will be guided and others whom you will need to meet will be guided unto you. Our beloved Son gave His life for you to understand your way into the Inner Kingdom, but what did you do? You made many religions out of Him, set Him apart upon an altar to worship. Are you to always misunderstand His teachings? His teachings were to free you, to bring you back to us. He said, *"I have come so ye will have life and have it more abundantly."* He also said, *"The truth shall set you free."*

You are not free going to your temples, synagogues and churches, following the religious rules and regulations of someone's limited mentalization of our Son's teachings. What a waste! You think you can chant, confess your errors, say a few learned prayers repeatedly and you have reached us? No, Dear Ones, you have not reached us, you have chased your own tail as a dog will do for exercise. You are exercising in futility. We are a presence, a peaceful presence with wisdom and love, Creation with transformation as part of the connection.

The gods of dark are happy and content. You have settled for the limitation of religion, which keeps you from connecting with the Kingdom of Heaven within you. It is prolonging their game. Go within, Dear Ones, come back to us.

Now, let us address the diet of death once again, Dear Ones. You as women, you as mothers, sisters, wives, daughters – there is an epidemic on Earth and this epidemic is being supported by the gods of dark. It is their basic weapon that they are using to prepare the children on Earth to become future alcoholics and drug addicts and it's SUGAR! Yes, Dear Ones, sugar is the main weapon that the gods of dark are using to create addictions.

Sugar's negative effects on the body:

1. Sugar can suppress the immune system.
2. Sugar upsets the minerals in the body.
3. Sugar causes hyperactivity, anxiety, difficulty concentrating and crankiness in children.
4. Sugar produces a significant rise in triglycerides.

5. Sugar contributes to the reduction in defense against bacterial infection.

6. Sugar can cause kidney damage.

7. Sugar reduces high density lipoproteins.

8. Sugar leads to chromium deficiency.

9. Sugar leads to cancer of the breasts, ovaries, intestines, prostrate and rectum.

10. Sugar increases fasting levels of glucose and insulin.

11. Sugar causes copper deficiency.

12. Sugar interferes with absorption of calcium and magnesium.

13. Sugar weakens eyesight.

14. Sugar raises the level of neurotransmitters called serotonin.

15. Sugar can cause hypoglycemia.

16. Sugar can produce an acidic stomach.

17. Sugar can raise adrenalin levels in children.

18. Sugar malabsorption is frequent in patients with dysfunctional bowel disease.

19. Sugar can cause aging.

20. Sugar can lead to alcoholism.

21. Sugar can cause tooth decay.

22. Sugar contributes to obesity.

23. High intake of sugar increases the risk of Crohn's Disease with ulcerative colitis.

24. Sugar can cause changes frequently found in persons with gastric or duodenal ulcers.

25. Sugar can cause arthritis.

26. Sugar can cause asthma.

27. Sugar can cause Candida albicans (yeast infections).

28. Sugar can cause gallstones.

29. Sugar can cause heart disease.

30. Sugar can cause appendicitis.

31. Sugar can cause multiple sclerosis.

32. Sugar can cause hemorrhoids.

33. Sugar can cause varicose veins.

34. Sugar can cause elevated glucose and insulin responses in oral contraceptive users.

35. Sugar can lead to periodontal disease.

36. Sugar can contribute to osteoporosis.

37. Sugar contributes to saliva acidity.

38. Sugar can cause a decrease in insulin sensitivity.

39. Sugar leads to decreased glucose tolerance.

40. Sugar can decrease growth hormone.

41. Sugar can increase cholesterol.

42. Sugar can increase the systolic blood pressure.

43. Sugar can cause drowsiness and decrease activity in children.

44. Sugar can cause migraine headaches.

45. Sugar can interfere with the absorption of protein.

46. Sugar causes food allergies.

47. Sugar can contribute to diabetes.

48. Sugar can cause toxemia during pregnancy.

49. Sugar can contribute to eczema in children.

50. Sugar can cause cardiovascular disease.

51. Sugar can impair the structure of DNA.

52. Sugar can change the structure of protein.

53. Sugar can make our skin age by changing the structure of collagen.

54. Sugar can cause cataracts.

55. Sugar can cause emphysema.

56. Sugar can cause atherosclerosis.

57. Sugar can promote and elevation of low density proteins (LDL)

58. Sugar can cause free radicals in the blood stream.

59. Sugar can cause hunger pains and overeating.

60. Sugar can cause to dementia.

This drug plays havoc with your auric shield and causes pain in the body, mood swings and negative behavior in children, lower IQ – intelligence quotation. It is the number one weapon of the dark and it comes in the disguise of a treat, a reward – ice cream, cookies, cake, and candy. Raise your children on fresh fruits and natural dried fruits for the sweetness of life. Take away the power of the gods of dark; take your children and family off of refined sugars. Give them life-force foods, which hold the life-force within them. Have you ever wondered why fresh picked fruits or vegetables taste so much better? Because they still hold the full force of the life-force!

Mother's you hold the key to the promised brotherhood and sisterhood of man and womankind in your hands; give your children life-force foods in a balanced diet.

A special note to foster mothers: the children you are caring for, whether in your home or an orphanage have been most likely nutritionally starved. Give them life-force foods. Find pure supplements to revitalize their little bodies and most of all teach them they have a Holy Mother and Father within them, whom love them unconditionally. Create the children of God, good, love. It is within your power.

We will speak now of a simple, but complex truth!

Dear Ones,

Spirit is all encompassing; it includes all living matter and souls. It is the life-force within all Creation. This Holy Spirit of Creation unites all!

Separatism divides, places barriers, and borders create hatred and misunderstandings. Race, religion, creed, gender, age, income, financial success or monetary limitation, wellness of the body or unwellness of the body, physical beauty, physical plainness, political beliefs, etc., these are all limited, negative opportunities to see separateness in your fellow man, woman or child.

This separateness is a lie. When Jesus said, *"Mother, brother, sister, we are all one in the same,"* this is what He was speaking of. Dear Ones recognize the truth, the Spirit that flows within you flows within all life. Stop playing mind games with yourselves. You are all part of the life-force. It is Creation. The beloved Creator is within all.

Go within and feel the creative power within you. Be at peace. Know the Creator is in you. You are part of the magnificent presence of the creative force called divine love.

When you go within and feel the presence of the divine love, fill up with that presence; then share that divine presence with the Earth and all her children. Think what will happen if all go within and connect with divine unconditional love, and then share it with the world. The Earth and all the inhabitants would experience Heaven on Earth; the Lion would lay down with the Lamb, peace on Earth, good will to all; a new Heaven within and a new heavenly Earth without wars. Hatred would cease. Borders would be a thing of the past. Separatism would no longer exist. Love would rule business, countries, and ideas. This is the plan Dear Ones, to bring love to Earth and all her children to transform consciousness. It shall be done.

Since Earth's measurement of time of the year of nineteen ninety-five, the Wheel of Karma or sowing and reaping has been in full effect for the souls sowing bad seeds. They are being taken off the planet or they have chosen an illness that reflects their misdeeds.

If they bore false witness against someone, they will experience the loss of communications in their last days. If they tried to control others through manipulation, they will lose their ability of freedom and end their days in a wheelchair. If they came from earthly ego, they will be humbled. If they have harmed or killed, they will experience the harm and if killed, they will take on the victim's karmic debts in a lower density than Earth. Mother Earth has served the children of God and the children of man, only the ones whom will honor her will be allowed to stay on Earth. Leaving Earth, making your transition to the other side, you will be placed in a restoring cocoon of healing love for the period of days you will require to repair. Then you appear before the Council of Light for you to be given permission to view your life on Earth. You will see your accomplishments and failures and then you will be assigned to your next experience. If you are one of the volunteer souls whom came to Earth without self karma, you will return to your Angelic Forces for a space of reflection and reunite with your soul family for a duration measured by your advancement of soul. Then you will choose your next assignment along with the Angelic Forces approval.

There are many volunteer souls on Earth whom are helping, healing, and transforming consciousness in their own way. We will address the volunteer souls in *Are You a Lightworker?*

The souls that have come to Earth to pay off their last age of karma have been given the opportunity to pay off their past life karmic debts. Take advantage of your opportunity to pay off your debts. With love, go within, serve, tithe to the needy, recognize the Source within all life and share the Source within you with others on Mother Earth. Become a child of God, good, love. Turn away from the dark and its pitfalls – the diet of death, pornography, materialism, greed, hatred, separatism, judgment, and earthly ego.

Go within, Dear Ones, we will carry you the rest of your journey in love.

There is no end, only the beginning of understanding the truth. For it shall set you free.

CHAPTER XIV

How to Go Within and Connect with Us

To connect with us, with the Kingdom of Heaven within you – make sure you are in a peaceful place without interruption. If you are at home, turn off the bells of your telephones, answering machines, etc.

Turn on soft meditational music. Find a comfortable chair or couch to sit on. Uncross your feet and arms. Take gentle, deep breaths. Feel the cleansing breath when inhaling. Recognize the release of cleansing your lungs and blood stream.

Softly, silently feel *"Every breath I take is the sacred breath within me."* Feel the sacred breath. Feel it spread through your lungs. Feel it spread slowly, peacefully through your body, starting with the chest area up through the throat, down through the hips, up to the top of your head. Then down through your legs ever so peacefully and slowly, and then you will acknowledge the presence within you. This presence will fill you. It will float into all levels of your body, mind and spirit, it will carry you. Now, feel a peaceful ball of love and light in the center of your heart and chest. Feel the ball of love and light expand slowly throughout your torso, spreading softly throughout your legs and feet. Now, feel this extra love and peace spread up through your throat to the top of your head and beyond.

Be patient with yourselves. Some of you will feel the presence instantly; others will take time. But you are worth the time. We will be there, please remember this.

Feel yourself float from your heart, the middle of your chest to your throat. Feel the throat release unwanted energy; allow the energy to flow into the unconditional energy of light and love.

When this is accomplished, feel yourself in the middle of your forehead. Allow yourself to release unwanted energy from your forehead, and then breathe in consciously the sacred breath into the middle of your forehead. Allow this loving, peaceful energy to go to the top of your head and feel the release of unwanted energy from this part of your body.

Feel the divine presence within you. You have come home. Welcome home, Dear Ones. It has been such a long time.

Now what?

Your body is the temple of the living God. Recognize this truth. This means you have the power within you to transform you and your life. And if you are a female, mother, daughter, sister, you may guide others to the inner power. If you would like more detailed information, refer to *Awakening to Your Inner Light*.

CHAPTER XV

Your Divine Self

This chapter will start with a few quotes from the Bible.

"Man – woman, know yourselves, ye are gods."

"What ever a man, woman thinks of him/herself, so is the man/woman."

"Ask and believe it shall be given unto you."

We hope you may see a pattern. The pattern is your thoughts, ideas or consciousness about yourself that creates your reality or experience. This is where you may change part of your reality.

If you are experiencing illness, start going within and visualize yourself feeling your cells repairing in your body. Tell the cells in your body that they are to be filled with the Creator's love and peace. Ask yourself what has this illness done for you? Does it give you more attention? Does it excuse you from responsibilities to others? Does it play out the victim consciousness so others will lend a helping hand or empathy?

When you do a soul search and find the answers, you may be programmed from an elder family member whom had health issues.

"The sins of the father fall upon the son." Meaning the consciousness or patterns of the parents is imprinted upon the children. Find your imprint, recognize it, then release it by saying, *"I bless, release and erase this limited, negative pattern that says I must be ill because..."* Then affirm *"I am filled with divine light and healing. Every cell of my body is whole, perfect and healed in the Light of God, good and love."*

Women you are the spiritual hope of the heavens. It is you whom have the ability to reach us. For most of you have set aside your earthly egos and realized you are a vessel to align with your highest selves.

Go within and guide your families to follow your example. Free yourself and your families of the diet of death. Nurture yourselves first, then your family. Realize we are here to support you. You will learn to trust the divine flow.

Chapter XVI

The Commandants

Let us discuss the true meaning of the Commandants. They are Divine Laws mistranslated. They should have been translated to say: *Thou cans't not* instead of *thou shall not* for the Divine Law of Sowing and Reaping is in effect.

You cannot gain from stealing because if you steal, you will be stolen from. Plus stealing is an affirmation in consciousness of poverty. It means you do not believe you are capable of manifesting the abundance to create your own good.

Now, envy is an affirmation of good for the one you envy and an affirmation for loss for you. Envy is a double-edged sword.

To bear false witness against another is to create a ripple effect into the Universe; to lie about another and in that lie you bring harm. You will pay dearly for that commandant, Dear Ones. Watch your words, they have power. May your power work for the Light. To love thy God with all thy might – we have explained this previously – it means to align with us for all time.

To keep the Sabbath is so misunderstood. It means to rest and to align with us. You need to care for your temple, your body, nurture and align with the Creator, your Holy Father and I, your Mother. Every day should express rest and alignment with us.

To go to a building, saying words out loud, dressing in your best clothes, repeating the same words, gossiping about other members, creating little groups of friends, excluding others – this is another abomination to us.

Align with your Inner Kingdom; fill yourself with the inner love and peace, then you will recognize the Light of Creation in all your fellow man, woman, child, animals, birds, trees, and flowers. Life is all Creation. Go within, connect into that Source; expand your horizons.

When your actions are positive, you send out positive reactions to the Universe and it will come back to you ten-fold. Expressing positive actions for gain or because it is expected of you, then your actions come from the mind and not the spirit and you will experience struggle and earthly hardships. When you go within, align with the unlimited Source within you, then your giving is aligned with the unlimited wisdom, love and peace and your giving and sharing will be supported by the very all, the Heavens, the Holy Spirit.

Chapter XVII

Tithing

Organized religion would have you believe you must tithe to them. The Law of Tithing works because it tells the Creator you trust in the Law of Sowing and Reaping. Casting your bread upon the waters. You have faith in the unlimited Source. Organized religion would have you believe that the church is the only place to tithe. This is a falsehood.

Tithing in its true self is a Divine Law, teaching you in the form of matter and consciousness. When you give out, it comes back to you ten-fold. It might be in the form of being a good listener to one in need or not listening to gossip about others.

A true tithing can be giving secretly to an organization with people in need, stopping to help another, sharing a smile, a word of encouragement when needed, a helping hand with a door and a sense of generosity of spirit to others. Always go within and see where the need is to be filled.

When you go within, you will be guided to the divine sharing and giving. Your Inner Kingdom will guide you. When you stand before the divine Source after your sojourn, you will take inventory of your abilities of giving and aligning with your God-self. Did you ignore the Inner Kingdom and struggle on your own? Was life difficult because you were not guided to allow the unlimited Source to help carry your burden?

Always go within, the unlimited Heavens will support and guide you.

CHAPTER XVIII

A Child of God versus the Child of Man

*E*ons and eons ago, man and womankind fell into greed and separation of spirit. They looked to the physical world for their pleasures. Greed, materialization and hatred became the expression of their consciousness. This created havoc on the planet they inhabited. The end result was great destruction of other planets. These planets are now referred to as black holes. These souls were split in twos, threes and more and they migrated to Eden, a garden created on Earth for intergalactic travelers. Many food and water supplies were grown on Earth. The growth on Earth became so overgrown that the children of God created animals on Earth to keep the vegetation on Earth under control.

Prior to your King James Bible, this was referred to in the Bible as 'the god's did this, the god's did that.' Paul said *"Man know yourselves, ye are Gods."*

These souls that split, entered into the lower form animal kingdom and became imbedded in lower form consciousness. The Angelic Realm sent the gods from a higher life form to cohabit with the souls imbedded in the lower animal forms.

"Go and procreate and do not spill thy seed upon thy soil."

The Roman government in the form of the Roman Catholic Church chose to twist that meaning in order to gain power and wealth. The more Catholics, the more they are able to rule.

We will explain the true meaning of go and procreate and do not spill thy seed upon thy soil. It was given to the Sons of God cohabiting with the Daughters of Man. This was a time when souls entered into lower forms of flesh on Earth, the primate form. Due to their worlds being destroyed by massive weapons, these souls were split and sought out life and found it on Earth. Earth was used as a garden for other worlds, referred to as the Blue Planet. The gods placed animals in the Garden of Eden to prevent overgrowth of the garden. The animals shared the food with the gods. When these worlds were destroyed by greed and misunderstanding of Divine Laws, it created a vacuum, you refer to them as Black Holes.

These souls whom experienced the shattering and split sought out life and ended up in the animal kingdom on Earth. The Masters of Higher Realm met with Mother Creator, your Holy Mother and I your Father, and we sent the sons of god to cohabit with the daughters of man in order to raise the species to a higher level. It could only be the Sons of God able to do this, for having the daughters of God cohabiting with the sons of man would mean our daughters of God would carry in their wombs a lower vibration child, understand?

Birth control today or the absence of birth control is strictly the Roman Church attempting to control you, in order to fill their pockets. The Catholic Church is one of the most corrupt organizations on Mother Earth.

"The daughters of man cohabited with the Sons of God." This was done several times to raise the species to a higher evolved being. To bring up the cell memory and consciousness back to God. It is so simple, Dear Ones. Go within, return to your God-selves. Come back to us. Be the unlimitedness of your soul and consciousness. This means the gifts of Heaven are within you.

What are the gifts of Heaven? Here's a list of some of the gifts:

- Unconditional love, unconditional peace, truth, and the wisdom to apply that truth.
- Creation on all levels.
- Divine friendships, divine unity, divine polarity mate, divine purpose and collaboration.

- Heavenly music.
- Healing and spiritually inspired art, writing, sculpture, etc.
- Growth of the plant kingdom beyond Earth's imagination.
- Divine prophecies, healing and divine wisdom.

You did not come to Earth alone, Dear Ones. Each and every one of you are assigned guides and Angels to guide and protect you. This will be referred to as a woman's intuition, a gut level feeling or a knowingness. Those of you whom know how to go within and reach your inner Heaven will be allowed to hear and feel our guidance. It is that small voice within filled with peace and understanding. Life is a game, either you become the unlimited child of God or you play out the limitation of the child of man.

Trust me, Dear Ones, the key to the unlimited game is to love your brother and sister animal. When you eat their flesh, you return to the time of the souls entering into the lower forms when the Sons of God had to cohabit with the daughters of man. By eating their flesh, you lower your frequency and join the animal kingdom's level of consciousness. This leaves you vulnerable to other forms of the lower form diet – caffeine, dairy, refined sugar, alcohol, drugs, sodas, colas and coffee –all killing your children and creating great suffering for them. You, as mothers, have the power to pull your children off this wheel of darkness. Please, Dear Ones, free yourselves and your children, return them to love, return them to the children of God, good, love and most of all return them to the divine ascension of their Higher-Self.

Dear Ones, your Bible has been tampered with, the Nicene and Ecumenical Council in the 1100 and 1200's removed information to keep you imprisoned to the Catholic Church. They removed the feminine polarity of your Holy Parents in order to control you. Feminine is to receive. They would deny you the ability of receiving from us, I your Mother and your Holy Father. They would have you go to their priests instead of us. This is an idolatry of the worst kind. They did it for greed.

The Spanish Inquisition created many atrocities until 1820 when it was abolished. This Church and some of its members have created darkness for their souls. They think they can hide behind their large organization and manifest evil. You whom have harmed a child in your black robes, misusing your power and have or think you have been spared punishment on Earth are mistaken; you will be in grief for eons in a lower form of existence. It will be carried out in a two-dimensional reality.

Woe unto those whom have misused their powers. *"Be ye aware of men who come in long black robes, in my name, they are but wolves in sheep clothing"* – *Christ.* In Our name, you will suffer for doing so. It is not us whom will punish you, but the Law of Sowing and Reaping you will answer to.

What are greed, hatred, separatism, and materialism? It is a belief that you are alone and that you can be greater or lesser than another and that you have only yourself to call upon in your hour of need. It is a belief that only material and earthly possessions are worthy of your attention. It is a belief that when you leave Mother Earth and die, you will no longer exist. It is a belief that this world is a dog-eat-dog existence. It is called the absence of divine love and unity with the divine universal unlimited Source.

This life is temporary, then you go on to the next existence and your past deeds follow you as part of your soul's frequency. You will be with souls of your own consciousness and frequency. Is this what you wish to create? To be with all souls whom are separate from love, good and Creation? Or do you choose to be with souls that share your divine purpose and existence?

You will see the churches fall in this lifetime. They have kept you from us long enough. Take back your power, come unto us, Dear Ones, and go within.

Eliminate carcinogens from your diet. Recognize the life-force within all living beings, including animals and plant life.

Let go of judging yourselves and others as separate. See the unity in all life.

CHAPTER XIX

The Valiant Ones (for Woman)

Your Holy Mother and I, your Father will tell you of these Valiant souls. They come to Earth with an inner dedication to be at their highest self when needed.

Some have joined your armed services, Peace Corps, the fire department; sheriff and police departments and others have become doctors, dentists, paramedics and teachers. These souls, whom have come to Earth with an inner drive of purpose, will rise to the highest acts of kindness and bravery when called upon to do so. There is a major unlimited energy force of good and love concentrated on Earth from the celestial beings at this time and many of her children of Valiant souls from our Creator have come to Earth to do their part. These souls will leave Earth without being affected by the Wheel of Death or Karma. Sometimes the Valiant Ones will take a job of earthly pursuits, such as being in service with utilities and repairs. These souls will lend a helping hand beyond what is expected of them and they will do it with care.

Finding these souls are easy if you live in a small community, but if you live in the city, they become obscure with the consciousness of anonymity.

There is such a dichotomy on Mother Earth at this time. The Light is rising with all the enlightened souls on Earth at this time, which is now creating the darkness to attack the Light. As mankind's consciousness awakens to the Light, it creates forms of darkness that attack the Light. We are seeing this today with terrorists all over the planet.

There is a purpose for this horrific darkness and that purpose is to bring all the children on Earth together and fulfill the prophecies. There shall be one world, one belief, and one people. The brotherhood and sisterhood of man and womankind are to be built out of joining forces against the evil that is being expressed today.

Children of Earth band together against this evil. It is the purpose of the evil, to bring you to the beginning of the brotherhood and sisterhood of man and womankind. The Valiant Ones are working towards this goal to bring healing, peace and love to Mother Earth.

CHAPTER XX

The Heavenly Conspiracy

Your Holy Mother and I, your Holy Father will now speak of the Heavenly Conspiracy. It has been taking place for over two hundred years now. We have sent you messengers to unveil the levels of truth in the teachings of Christ. These teachers taught the power of thought, which Christ taught, but He taught so much more that created churches and courses for these unveilings. These teachings taught you to use thought for manifestation.

"What ever you think, so you are."

But He also asked you to honor your father and mother. This means to go within and align with us, your Holy Parents – to become a part of us in consciousness; a consciousness that rises above all limitation of worry, fear, anger, hatred, prejudices, and greed.

Christ asked you to love one another. Many have tried this with earthly love. What Christ meant was to recognize the life-force in all and know you are one with that life-force.

We have so many volunteers on Earth, souls whom have come to Earth to help bring you home to us. There are the growers of organic fruits, seeds, nuts and vegetables, Health Food stores and pure vitamins and supplements. Some are purifying water to heal. Musicians are composing harmonic music to heal your body, mind and spirit. Chiropractors, acupuncture and acupressure, herbalists, pure essential oils, cell salts, teachers of inner connecting prayers, spiritual massage therapists, healers, teachers, intuitive counselors – all are here to empower you and bring you back to us, to love, to the eternal Light of Creation. Artists bring in etherical paintings and colors. Writers channeling the truth to bring you back to the Source, to us, your Holy Mother Creator, your Mother God and I, your Father. You have men and women working with energy. Some of you must learn to bring in the unlimited energy from the Creator so you will not deplete your personal energy.

There is an unlimited energy supply awaiting you. Go within and tap into the unlimited Source.

Let us address the volunteer souls whom are still limited or asleep to their mission on Earth. Some of you will feel like there is something you must accomplish on Earth. You may be confused as to what that might be. Go within and call upon us your Holy Parents, we will guide you. Be patient, the answer will come.

Clean up your diet – eliminate carcinogens from your diet. Follow the diet of life. Pray. Do service to the less fortunate. Lend a helping hand to those in need. Listen to the inner voices, the small voice within will always be loving.

If you have a challenge, or are hearing the voice's of the dark, then follow the diet of life and seek a trustworthy healer to help free you from the dark.

There are many volunteer souls whom are on Earth and are suffering from addiction. Why, you ask??? Because, they have forgotten why they came to Earth and they feel the density of Earth is too heavy, so they take drugs to keep their bodies thin or they take drugs to stop the helpless and hopeless feeling they have, attempting to survive on Earth.

First, if you are one of these souls captured by the dark – turn off your television; eliminate meat, dairy, tobacco, processed sugar, caffeine, and alcohol from your diet. Find a chiropractor, an enlightened one please and a masseuse working with the healing Light to work on your body. Go within and bless, release and erase the need for the addition and request the Light of love to come into your body. The guides you came to Earth with are standing by to help you return to your enlighten self.

Volunteers are here to bring their brothers and sisters home. Home to unconditional love and peace that surpasses all earthly understanding. Why would they volunteer to come to Earth? They come to Earth for you, dear children! Because they have watched you suffer on the Wheel of Karma and observe you repeating the Wheel of Karma over and over and over again.

They are souls whom have risen above the Wheel and have a magnitude of compassion for your suffering. They are referred to in your Bible as the Chosen Ones. These are the souls whom have agreed to come to Earth to heal and clear your karma and suffering.

These souls are the most dedicated, honored and appreciated in Higher Realm. They have left their higher existence to come to a lower existence and experience your karma and struggle, until they found the answer to clear and heal all the earthly limited, negative karma.

These volunteers work daily to free you from your limitations. The great spiritual conspiracy is to return you to us, Dear Ones.

Chapter XXI

Sins of the Father Fall upon the Son (for Woman)

"*The sins of the father fall upon the son*," a quote from the Bible that translates to: the programming of the parents is passed down to their children.

This truth is overlooked or it is also greatly misunderstood. Your Holy Mother and I, your true Father, will explain this to you. Our purpose in doing so is to free you from all earthy limitations and addictions.

First, your soul will be drawn to the parents you are assigned to. This is to work out the past debts the parents and child may have to complete. Then the child will be programmed from the womb regarding the father and mother's consciousness during the pregnancy. This consciousness or programming will be passed on to the child. If the pregnancy was not planned or the child unwanted, the infant will be imprinted with that consciousness as well. This is why many adopted children have a feeling of not being loved from the very beginning. They will sometimes seek out their birth mother or father to resolve this unwanted programming. Most times they end up disappointed.

There are also the limited, negative patterns the parents have received from their parents, so the child must overcome all these limited, negative programs. To overcome this programming, you do so by releasing these negative patterns and returning to us, your true parents – Mother-Father God.

Your Holy Mother and I, your Father wish to address addictions of relationships. If you are in an addictive relationship with a toxic mate, you need to return in your mind's eye to your parent's behavior and patterns. *"The sins of the father fall upon the son."*

The patterns, be they negative or positive are imprinted upon you. If your mate is toxic and you feel compelled to stay in the dysfunctional relationship, then you are playing out your parent's patterns. It has nothing to do with love. It is reliving negative patterns of your parents in your life. Your feeling of love is a compulsion to relive your parent's patterns.

Go back in time and release the negative patterns. See yourself blessing your parents with God's healing Light. Pour it over your parents, and then pour it over you. Fill yourself with our divine love. Trust you are worthy of a love – a pure love.

Fill your heart and body with our love. We will repair your belief system into ascending to a higher level of consciousness by blessing, releasing and erasing the limited, negative programming you have received from your parents.

You are worthy of a divine love, heaven sent.

Know you are enough.

You are whole, total and complete. The Kingdom of Heaven is within you.

CHAPTER XXII

The Dark (for Woman)

The dark is only the absence of Light. The gods of dark came into existence when they became restless of being the Gods of Light, the Sons of God. These gods turned their consciousness away from the Light. The further away from the Light, the darker the gods of dark became. These gods played their games in the astral realm until they took their game to lower realms. The results were greed, corruption, murder, mayhem, wars, and atrocities, ending and destroying many levels of consciousness and other worlds. These worlds were obliterated, creating black holes in the Universe.

The gods of dark's games are coming to an end. The Light has gathered together in order to end the dark's influence on Mother Earth and the eternal Universe.

These gods have created so much misery and havoc. Their sowings will now close in on them. They will have to answer to the heavens. The laws of karma will end the gods of dark's game sooner than anyone knows or will even realize. For our Son of Light and Love made a promise to the children of Earth – He will return and walk the Earth for over a thousand years. There shall be peace on Earth and good will towards men.

Now, we will tell you how you can free yourselves and your family from the control and corruption of the dark to help bring the peace on Earth and good will towards men, as prophesized by our Son.

We will show you how you may end the gods of dark's control. The gods of dark control man and womankind's consciousness through eating of the Tree of Knowledge of Good and Evil. You were told this in your very first book – Genesis.

Even though your Bible has been tampered with, the sentence is still intact. Adam and Eve were thrown out of the Garden of Eden because they ate of the Tree of Knowledge of Good and Evil. The operative word being ate!

Very few children of Earth have realized the in-depth meaning of this statement. We will give you all the levels of control that the gods of dark use for their control and their games. These next pages will be devoted to freeing mankind from the control of the dark – your diet – what you eat, drink and take into your body can be filled with the energy of the Creator or the lack of energy, meaning dead flesh (meat), dairy, alcohol, sugar, drugs, cigarettes, chewing tobacco, caffeine, and bleached flour. All these things are attached to the dark (the gods of dark). When you eat a carcinogen, it places a crack in your auric shield. This allows the attachment to enter your shield and feed off your body and mind.

These attachments are black reptilian, vine-like attachments – lower forms of evil that attach and feed off of you, controlling you and keeping you addicted. All humans addicted to carcinogens are being controlled by the dark.

We observe our children fighting these addictions. We see these lower form attachments strangling some of you. These attachments cause personality changes.

The most destructive addiction causing element you are feeding to your children is sugar. Parents STOP giving your children sugar. It is filled with bleach. It places a crack in your children's auric shield and they become agitated and hyperactive. Sugar addiction leads to alcohol and drug addiction.

Give them all organic, non-heated honey, pure maple syrup, agave, xylitol, barley and rice syrup in small amounts. Let them enjoy fruit as their sweetener. Please protect your children from the dark!

Every drag off a cigarette allows the dark into your lungs, nose cavity, skin, hair, eyes, even your third eye. The creatures that follow the dark are of the lowest form of consciousness and you are inviting them into your body! Think about it.

Meat! You are eating a dead body of a murdered animal. Thou shall not kill!! When you eat dead flesh, the dark entities that feed off the dead will enter your body with the killed animal. Beware this is the dark at its very best – a sales pitch – steaks, hamburgers, drumsticks, and roasts are all camouflage for dead, murdered animals.

Alcohol has sometimes been referred to as spirits, coming from the dark spirits whom would be drawn to the alcohol. Have you not witnessed a personality change in a person under the influence of alcohol?!

You have the power to do your part in ending the game of dark on Earth. Drink pure water; eat organic fruits, vegetables, seeds, nuts and grains.

Walk away from all carcinogens:

1. Alcohol
2. Sugar
3. Tobacco
4. Meat
5. Dairy (animal)
6. Drugs
7. Deep-fried foods

Go within and align with us, your Holy Parents. If drugs are required for a much needed operation find the least offensive one to you. Then after your surgery, cleanse your body through diet and prayer. Eventually, you will have non-evasive surgery, so drugs will no longer be needed.

Pray when going into surgery. Ask God, the Light and Angels to surround you for protection. Let go of all anger. Anger is a tool of the dark. The gods of dark celebrate in your anger. To express anger is to say you are separate from your good, your God or love – are all one and the same.

Be at peace and know the Light has dominion over the dark. Join the children of Light now. End the game of dark. Bring love, peace, forgiveness, and healing to Mother Earth and all her children. It only takes one hundred and forty-four thousand to turn the tide. Have you have asked yourself 'What may I do?'

This we ask of you. Turn to us, your Holy Mother and Father; we are awaiting your return.

CHAPTER XXIII

Prophecies for the Future (for Woman)

During the holidays, the winter solstice, all of you should be doing less activity – do pampering things, self-nurturing, healing teas and soups, saunas, massages, body cleansings, resting and nurturing, instead of celebrating the holidays by the control of the dark with sugar, meat, dairy, and alcohol.

This conspiracy was created by the dark in the time of Rome and laid out to weaken the child of God instead of renewing and strengthening them, making them vulnerable, at the mercy to the control of the dark by celebrating in the middle of the winter solstice.

We are going to give you a visual picture of what the future will look like – your work day will be no longer than 4-hours a day, 6 at the very most, over 80 percent of the workforce will work out of their homes, and a major shift in the workforce will work for pleasure instead of monetary gain, resulting in more abundance for them personally. For where you love, you will be abundant. The film and food industry will do 4-hour shifts. Travel will be cut down to a bare minimum and life-force foods will grow at your fingertips in your home.

There will be scientific machines brought to Mother Earth that will align with acupuncture points and release blockages within your bodies. This will bring in your balanced Chi and align you so you can meditate correctly and you will feel renewed. It will be a common occurrence to wake up in the morning after your body eliminating from the day before, you merging and aligning with us, Mother-Father God and Higher Realm. We will communicate with you as to what this day shall hold. Be prepared for spiritual creativity and alignment to reign throughout your day, both work and play.

We, in the Heavens (Higher Realm), celebrate play, joy and euphoria every day. The children on Earth have felt this compelling energy to accomplish success; however they have been misdirected in these accomplishments. Before you come to Earth, you realize you may accomplish more on Earth than in the heavens (astral plane), for one good deed on Earth is worth one hundred thousand on the astral or heavenly planes. As you come to Earth and go into the land of nod, your cell memory is not quite clear, so you have a sense of urgency to accomplish, complete, and do. However, all we have asked for all of you to remember is to love God with all your heart and mind, love one another, and to serve man and womankind. While many of you are running around accruing wealth, world recognition (fame), properties, automobiles and mechanical toys, the real purpose for you to come to Earth is to love – this is recognizing the spirit in all life forms on Earth, including yourselves.

Choose God and Love over judgment, bigotry, hatred and separation. Choose unity, spirit recognition, the brotherhood and sisterhood of man and womankind and serve one another with a joyful heart. Return Mother Earth to her healthy, loving state, you originally found her.

Your Holy Parents, Mother-Father God.

About the Author

Nancy R. Griffin's profession as an intuitive counselor began in 1983. Her intuitive gifts led to the discovery of her ability to heal illnesses in the body, mind and spirit from past life cell memory working in conjunction with holistic doctors. Additionally, she is connected to the Angelic Realm, the Christ Consciousness, Mother-Father God, Space Brothers and Sisters, the Ashtar Command and the White Robed Masters. Out of her creative flow came two metaphysical television cable shows. Upon requests from her students came many books covering all her teachings, including how to channel (Awakening to Your Inner Light) and others giving the divine laws for health, success, happiness, and peace.

Nancy continues to channel books from her home in a small mountain community in Southern California.